EVERYDAY JAPANESE

● EVERYDAY JAPANESE *A Basic English-Japanese Wordbook*

by Eldora S. Thorlin, M.A.
and Noah S. Brannen, PH.D.

New York · WEATHERHILL · *Tokyo*

First edition, 1969
Twenty-fourth printing, 1994

Published by Weatherhill, Inc.,
of New York and Tokyo, with editorial offices at
420 Madison Avenue, 15th Floor, New York, N.Y. 10017.
Protected by copyright under the terms of the
International Copyright Union; all rights reserved.
Printed in the U.S.A.

LCC CARD No. 69-19854
ISBN 0-8348-0037-3

CONTENTS

AUTHORS' INTRODUCTION

This dictionary takes its form from the need for a ready reference to Japanese words and expressions useful in day-to-day living to the foreign resident in Japan.

A valuable tool, language can open doors for its user, and even a slight fluency can break down barriers to mutual understanding. Our aim in compiling this dictionary has been to help, primarily but not exclusively, the resident foreigner in Japan take the first step forward in learning to "get along" in conversational Japanese. This book can help him through social difficulties and can aid him in developing a limited fluency in Japanese.

Users of our dictionary will not fail to note the high proportion of English loanwords found in its pages. This is accounted for by (1) the fast rate of importation of English words into the everyday speech of the Japanese today, and (2) the need to help beginners in Japanese achieve communication quickly and effectively.

Bearing in mind the nature and scope of our dictionary and the complexities of the Japanese language, we have restricted ourselves to only a brief explanation of pronunciation, grammar, and sentence structure.

Pronunciation

Japanese is not especially difficult to pronounce, but please note the following:

SHORT VOWELS

a as in f*a*ther   *e* as in y*e*s
i as in mach*i*ne   *o* as in s*o*lo
u as in r*u*le

LONG VOWELS

ā   *ei* (or *ē*)
ii (or *ī*)   *ō*
ū

Hold the long sounds at least twice as long as the short ones and don't let the sound change from start to finish.

When two vowels occur together in a word, let the pure quality of each one be heard, one after the other.

You may hear native speakers dropping the vowels *i* and *u* (especially the latter in the word *desu*) as shown here:

I like sukiyaki.
Watashi wa s'kiyaki ga s'ki des'. (dropped *u*'s)

He worked in the northern branch office.
K'ta no sh'ten de hatarakimash'ta. (dropped *i*'s)

You can learn to do this by imitating, but it is also permissible to retain these sounds as written in this book.

Except for some very special instances, every syllable in Japanese gets the same rhythm count and the same stress.

CONSONANTS

1. When the Japanese *r* appears within a word, pronounce it like the "dd" in the name "Eddy." When the *r* appears as

the first letter of a word, pronounce it like the English "r" but flick your tongue lightly against the roof of your mouth just behind your teeth.

2. The pronunciation of the Japanese *f* is best described as being like the "h" at the beginning of the English words "hoot," "hooligan," and "Hoover."

3. *G* is always hard as in "girl" and "glass."

4. The Japanese *h* before *i* is most closely pronounced like a harsh "sh" as in "ship."

5. The Japanese *ts* (used only in the syllable *tsu*) is like the italicized part of this sentence, "Let's sue him."

6. When *n* is followed by a raised dot (as in *bon·yari*), it is pronounced like the middle sound in the English word "singer."

Grammar

We have purposely omitted listing infinitives in the dictionary, restricting all verb entries to inflected forms found in sentences. Japanese verbs are highly flexible and bear a complex linguistic workload, the explanation of which is beyond the scope of this book.

Unlike their English equivalents, Japanese verbs do not have different forms to express person or number. Thus the verb form *arukimasu* can mean: I walk, you (singular or plural) walk, he (she, it) walks, we walk, they walk.

With only a few exceptions Japanese nouns do not show number, e.g., *hon* can mean "a book" or "the books."

ADJECTIVES

You will note that some entries are followed by *na* or *no*, e.g., *hen na* (strange) and *kara no* (empty) while others like *chiisai* (small) stand alone. Note how they are used:

He's small.
Kare wa chiisai desu.

He's a small man.
Kare wa chiisai otoko desu.

She's strange.
Kanojo wa hen desu.

She's a strange woman.
Kanojo wa hen na onna desu.

That box is empty.
Sono hako wa kara desu.

That is an empty box.
Sore wa kara no hako desu.

Sentence Structure

The verb in a Japanese sentence or clause appears at the end, so that the grammatical order follows this formula:

subject + object + verb

as in this sentence:

Kanojo wa akai sukāto o haite imasu.
 She   red   skirt   wearing is.
She is wearing a red skirt.

and this sentence:

Kanojo wa akai sukāto o haite imasen.
 She   red   skirt   wearing isn't.
She isn't wearing a red skirt.

Interrogative sentences are constructed by adding the particle *ka* after the verb. Thus we get:

Kanojo wa akai sukāto o haite imasu ka?
  She   red   skirt   wearing is?

Is she wearing a red skirt?

Because the Japanese counting system is frustratingly complicated, we have limited number entries to those of Japanese origin since these can be used to count most things in amounts from 1 to 10. Numbers and counting, however, are taken up in the section by that name on pages 163–67.

The authors wish to express their appreciation to Mrs. Kay Niiya for her invaluable help in the preparation of this dictionary.

EVERYDAY JAPANESE

LIST OF ABBREVIATIONS

fem.	feminine
J.	Japanese or Japanese-style
masc.	masculine
mil.	military
RR	railroad
W.	Western or Western-style

THE BASIC WORDBOOK

A

abacus *soroban*

above ... *no ue ni*

abscess *kanō*

absent-minded *bon·yari*

absorbent cotton *dasshi-men*

accelerator (car) *akuseru*

accent *akusento*
> Your a. is very good. *Anata no hatsuon wa ii desu.*

accident *jiko*
> car a. *jidōsha-jiko*

account: charge a. *tsuke*
> checking a. *tōza yokin*
> expense a. *kōsai-hi; hitsuyō keihi*
> savings a. *futsū yokin*
> time-deposit a. *teiki yokin*

accountant *kaikeishi*

accurate *seikaku na*

ace (playing card) *ēsu*

acne *nikibi*

across the street *michi no mukō*

active *katsudōteki na*

actor *haiyū*

actress *joyū*

address *jūsho*
> Give me your name and a. *O-namae to go-jūsho o o-negai shimasu.*
> Here's my name and a. *Kore wa watashi no namae to jūsho desu.*

address book *jūsho roku*

Address this in kanji, please. *Kono atena o kanji de kaite kudasai.*

adequate *tekitō na*

adhesive tape *bansōkō*

adjacent (to) *tonari no*

admission fee *nyūjōryō*
adopted child *yōshi* (m.),
  yōjo (f.)
adult *otona*
adventure *bōken*
adventurous *bōkenteki na*
advertisement *kōkoku*
afraid: Are you a.? *Kowai
  desu ka?*
  Don't be a. *Kowagaru koto
    wa nai.*
  I'm a. (scared). *Watashi
    wa kowai desu.*
  I'm not a. *Watashi wa ko-
    waku nai.*
afternoon *gogo*
  during the a. *gogo ni*
  Good a.! *Konnichi wa!*
  this a. *kyō no gogo*
  tomorrow a. *ashita no gogo*
  yesterday a. *kinō no gogo*
afterward *ato de*
After you! *Dōzo o-saki ni!*
again *mata*
  Do it a. *Mata shite kudasai.*
  Don't do it a. *Kore kara
    wa shinai yō ni.*
against ... *ni taishite*
ago: an hour a. *ichijikan mae*
  a minute a. *ippun mae*
  a month a. *ikkagetsu mae*

a short time a. *sukoshi mae*
a week a. *isshūkan mae*
a year a. *ichinen mae*
long a. *mukashi*
agree: Do you a.? *Sō omoimasu ka?*
  I a. *Sō omoimasu.*
  I don't a. *Sō omoimasen.*
ahead *saki*
  Go a. (Continue.) *Tsuzu-
  kete kudasai.*
  Who's a.? *Dotchi ga katte
  imasu ka?*
air *kūki*
air-conditioned *reibō no*
air conditioner *reibōki*
air conditioning *reibō-sōchi*
air letter *eā-retā*
airline *kōkū-gaisha*
airline terminal (building)
  eā-tāminaru
airmail *kōkūbin*
  via a. *kōkūbin de*
airmail stamp *kōkū-kitte*
airman (mil.) *kūgun-gunjin*
air mattress *eā-mattoresu*
airplane *hikōki*
airport *kūkō*
airsickness *hikōki-yoi*
airtight *mippei shita*
ajar *hambiraki*

à la carte *arakaruto*

alarm clock *mezamashi-dokei*

alcohol *arukŏru*
  rubbing a. *arukŏru*

alcoholic (an) *arukŏruchŭ-
doku kanja*

alien (an) *gaikokujin*

alien registration booklet
  *gaikokujin tŏroku shŏmei-
sho*

alike: They're both alike.
  Ryŏhŏ tomo nite imasu.

alimony *fujoryŏ*

alive: He (she) is still a.
  Mada ikite imasu.
  Is he (she) still a? *Mada
  ikite imasu ka?*
  Is it a.? *Ikite imasu ka?*
  It's a. *Ikite imasu.*

all (of it) *zembu*

all (of them) *minna*

allergic *arerugī-sei no*
  Are you a. to it? *Anata wa
  sore ni arerugī-sei desu
  ka?*
  I'm a. to it. *Sore ni arerugī-sei desu.*
  I'm not a. to it. *Sore ni
  arerugī-sei de wa arimasen.*

allergy *arerugī*

alley *roji*

alligator (leather) *wanigawa*

allowance (stipend) *kozukai*

all ready: It's a. r. *Jumbi ga
  dekimashita.*

all right *daijŏbu*
  Is it a. r.? *Daijŏbu desu ka?*
  It's a. r. *Daijŏbu desu.*

All right! (I agree!) *Yoroshii!*

all together (of persons)
  minna de

almond *āmondo*

almost *hotondo*

alone (by oneself) *hitori de*
  Are you a.? *O-hitori desu
  ka?*
  I'm alone. *Hitori desu.*
  I'm not alone. *Hitori de
  wa arimasen.*

alongside ... *no soba de*

aloud *koe o dashite*

already *mŏ*

also *mata*

aluminum foil (cooking)
  kukkingu-hoiru

always *itsu mo*

a.m. *gozen*

ambassador *taishi*

ambitious *yashinteki na*

ambulance *kyūkyūsha*
America *Amerika*
American (citizen) *Amerikajin*
American (made in America) *Amerika no*
American Embassy *Amerika taishikan*
American Express Credit Card *Amerikan Ekisupuresu Kurejitto-kādo*
ammonia *ammonia*
among ... *no naka ga*
amount (total) *gōkei*
amusement park *yūenchi*
anesthesia *masui*
under a. *masui-chū*
anesthetic *masui*
general a. *zenshin-masui*
local a. *kyokusho-masui*
angel cake *enjeru-kēki*
angry *okotta*
Are you a.? *Okorimashita ka?*
Don't be a. *Okoranai de kudasai.*
I'm a. *Watashi wa okotte imasu.*
I'm not a. *Watashi wa okotte imasen.*
animal *dōbutsu*

ankle *ashikubi*
I have a sprained a. *Ashikubi o nenza shimashita.*
anniversary: wedding a. *kekkon-kinembi*
another one (different) *betsu no mono*
another one (more) *mō hitotsu*
antifreeze *anchi-furīzu*
antihistamine *kō-hisutamin*
antiseptic (an) *bōfuzai*
anxious *shimpai de*
any *nani ka*
anyone *dare ka*
anything *nani ka*
Anything else? *Sono hoka ni nani ka?*
anyway *tomokaku*
anywhere *doko ka*
apart: It came a. *Barabara ni narimashita.*
apartment *apāto*
furnished a. *kagutsuki-apāto*
apartment building *apāto*
appendectomy *mōchō shujutsu*
appendicitis *mōchōen*
appetizers (hors d'oeuvres) *ōdoburu*

apple *ringo*
apple juice *appuru-jūsu*
apple pie *appuru-pai*
appointment *yakusoku*
apricot *anzu*
  dried a. *hoshi anzu*
April *Shi-gatsu*
apron *epuron*
arcade *ākēdo*
arch (in front of shrine) *tori-i*
architect *kenchikuka*
argue: Don't a., please. *Giron shinai de kudasai.*
arm *ude*
armchair *hijikake-isu*
armpit *waki no shita*
around (nearby) *sugu chikaku ni*
around: Turn a., please. *U-shiro o mukinasai.*
around the corner *kado o magatta tokoro*
arranged marriage *miai-kekkon*
arrive: What time does it a.? *Nanji ni tsukimasu ka?*
  When did you a.? *Nanji ni tsukimashita ka?*
arriving: What time are you a.? *Anata wa nanji ni tsukimasu ka?*
art *bijutsu*
art gallery *garō*
artificial respiration *jinkō-kokyū*
artist *geijutsuka*
ashtray *haizara*
Ask him (**her**). *Kare (kanojo) ni kikinasai.*
Asia *Ajia*
asleep He (she) is a. *Nete imasu.*
  He (she) is not a. *Nete imasen.*
  My foot's a. *Shibire ga kiremashita.*
asparagus *asuparagasu*
aspirin *asupirin*
as soon as possible *dekiru dake hayaku*
astringent (lotion) *asuto-rinzen*
Atlantic Ocean *Taiseiyō*
attendant: gas station a. *gasorin-sutando no jū-gyōin*
attic *yaneura-beya*
attractive *miryokuteki na*
August *Hachi-gatsu*
aunt (his, her, your) *obasan*
  (my) *oba*

Australia *Ōsutoraria*
Australian (citizen) *Ōsuto-rariajin*
Australian (made in Australia) *Ōsutoraria no*
Australian Embassy *Ōsutoraria taishikan*
author *sakka*
automatic *jidōteki na*
automatic transmission *ōtomachikku toransumisshan*

auto mechanic *jidōsha-shū-rikō*
automobile *jidōsha*
autumn *aki*
average *heikin*
  above a. *heikin ijō*
  below a. *heikin ika*
awake: Are you a.? *Okite imasu ka?*
  I'm a. *Okite imasu.*
awning *hiyoke*
azalea *tsutsuji*

B

baby *akambō*
baby bottle *honyūbin*
baby carriage *ubaguruma*
baby sitter *komori* (see also p. 160, Instructions for Child Care)
bachelor *dokushinsha*
back (reverse side) *ushiro*
  in b. of ... *no ushiro ni*
back (part of the body) *senaka*
back: I'm b. (in the house)! *Tadaima!*

  Let's go b. *Kaerimashō.*
  When will you be b.? *Itsu kaerimasu ka?*
back door *katte-guchi*
backside (buttocks) *o-shiri*
backup light *bakku-rampu*
backward (direction) *ushiro no hō*
back yard *uraniwa*
bacon *bēkon*
bacon & eggs *bēkon-eggu*
bad *warui*
bad habit *warui kuse*

bad luck *aku-un*
badminton *badominton*
bad-tempered *iji no warui*
bag *fukuro*
   a b. of ... *hitofukuro*
   paper b. *kami-bukuro*
   tea b. *tī-baggu*
baggage *tenimotsu*
   excess b. *chōka-tenimotsu*
bait *esa*
baked ham *hamu no maru-yaki*
baked potato *yaki-jagaimo*
bakery *pan·ya*
baking dish *ōbun·yō-fuka-zara*
baking powder *bēkingu-paudā*
baking soda (bicarbonate) *jūso*
balance due *zankin*
balcony *barukonī*
balcony seat *barukonī-shīto*
bald: He's b. *Atama ga hagete imasu.*
ball *bōru*
   a b. of ... *hitomaki*
   a baseb. *bōru*
   bowling b. *bōringu-bōru*
   golf b. *gorufu-bōru*
   tennis b. *tenisu-bōru*

   volley b. *barē-bōru*
ball (dance) *dansu-pātī*
balloon *fūsen*
ball-point pen *bōru-pen*
bamboo *take*
bamboo pole (for drying clothes) *monohoshi-zao*
bamboo shoots *take-no-ko*
banana *banana*
band (orchestra) *bando*
bandage *hōtai*
bandana *sukāfu*
bangs (hair) *o-kappa*
bank (of a river) *dote*
bank (commercial establishment) *ginkō*
bankbook *yokin-tsūchō*
bar: a bar of ... *ichimai*
bar (serving liquor) *bā*
barbershop *tokoya* (see also p. 150, At the Barber-shop)
barbiturate *barubitāru-zai*
bare *hadaka no*
barefooted *suashi no*
bargain (a good buy) *hori-dashi-mono*
bar hostess *bā no hosutesu*
barracks *heiei*
bartender *bāten*
base (mil.) *kichi*

off b. *kichi no soto de*
on b. *kichi no naka de*
baseball (a) *bōru*
baseball game *yakyū*
baseball glove *gurōbu*
baseball park *yakyūjō*
baseball stadium *yakyūjō*
basement *chikashitsu*
bashful *hazukashigari na*
Don't be b. *Hazukashi-garanai de kudasai.*
basket *kago*
wasteb. *kuzukago*
bassinet *yurikago*
bath *o-furo*
public b. *sentō*
sauna b. *sauna-buro*
Turkish b. *Toruko-buro*
bathing cap *kaisui-bō*
bathing suit *mizugi*
bath mat *basu-matto*
bathrobe *gaun*
bathroom *furoba*
bathroom sink *semmendai*
bath towel *basu-taoru*
bathtub *furo-oke*
batter (cooking) *neriko*
battery (car) *batterī*
storage b. *chikudenchi*
battery (flashlight) *denchi*
beach *kaigan*

beads (necklace) *kubikazari*
beam: high b. *uwamuki-raito*
low b. *shitamuki-raito*
beans (dried) *mame*
string b. *saya-ingen*
bean sprouts *moyashi*
beard *hige*
beater (whisk) *awatateki*
beautiful *utsukushii*
beauty operator *biyōshi*
beauty shop *biyōin* (see also p. 149, At the Beauty Shop)
Be careful! *Ki o tsukete!*
because *nazenara*
becoming: Is it b.? *Ni-ai-masu ka?*
It's not very b. *Amari yoku ni-aimasen.*
It's very b. *Yoku ni-aima-su.*
bed *beddo*
double b. *daburu-beddo*
double-decker bunks *ni-dan-beddo*
single b. *shinguru-beddo*
twin b. *tsuin-beddo*
bedding *shingu*
bed linen (sheets & pil-lowcases) *shītsu to maku-*

    ra-kabā

bedridden *netakiri no*

bedroom *shinshitsu*

bed sheet *shītsu*

bedspread *beddo-kabā*

bee *hachi*

beef *gyūniku*

    corned b. *kōn-bīfu*

    ground b. *gyū-hiki-niku*

    roast b. *rōsuto-bīfu*

beef bouillon *bīfu-buiyon*

beef liver *gyū-rebā*

beefsteak *bifuteki*

beer *bīru*

    a bottle of b. *bīru ippon*

    a glass of b. *bīru ippai*

    bottled b. *binzume-bīru*

    draft b. *nama-bīru*

beer glass *bīru-gurasu*

beet *bītsu*

beginning (the) *hajime*

Behave yourself! (to a child) *Otonashiku shinasai!*

behind ... *no ushiro ni*

behind (backside) *o-shiri*

belch *okubi*

bell: doorb. *yobirin*

bellboy *bōi*

below ... *no shita ni*

belt *beruto*

belt buckle *bakkuru*

bench *benchi*

Be patient! *Gaman shinasai!*

Be quick! *Hayaku!*

Be quiet! *Shizuka ni shinasai!*

berth: lower b. *gedan*

    upper b. *jōdan*

best (the) *ichiban ii*

    It's the b. *Ichiban ii desu.*

best man (wedding attendant) *hanamuko tsuki-soinin*

best seller (book) *besuto-serā*

better: Are you feeling b.? *Go-kibun wa mō ii desu ka?*

    Do you feel b.? *Go-kibun wa ii desu ka?*

    I feel b. *Daibu ii hō desu.*

    That's b. *Zutto ii desu.*

    Which one is b.? *Dotchi ga ii desu ka?*

between ... *no aida ni*

bias binding *baiasu-tēpu*

bib (child's) *yodare-kake*

Bible *Seisho*

bicarbonate of soda *jūsō*

bicycle *jitensha*

bicycle riding *saikuringu*

bid (bridge) *seri-ne*

bifocals *nishōten-renzu*

big *ōkii*

   too b. *ōki-sugimasu*

bill (account) *seikyūsho*

binding: bias b. *baiasu-tēpu*

   ski b. *sukī no shimegu*

binoculars *sōgankyō*

bird *tori*

birdcage *torikago*

birth certificate *shussei-shōmeisho*

birthday *tanjōbi*

   Happy b.! *O-tanjōbi ome-detō!*

   My b. is on … *Watashi no tanjōbi wa … desu.*

   When is your b.? *Anata no tanjōbi wa itsu desu ka?*

birthday party *tanjō-pātī*

birthmark *aza*

biscuit *bisuketto*

bite: Does he (the dog) b.? *Inu wa kamitsukimasu ka?*

   Be careful. He b. *Kami-tsuku kara, ki o tsukete kudasai.*

bitter (taste) *nigai*

black *kuroi*

black & white film *shiro-kuro fuirumu*

black coffee *burakku-kōhī*

blackhead *kuro-nikibi*

bladder *bōkō*

blade (knife, razor, tool) *ha*

blame: I don't b. you. *Anata ga warui no de wa arimasen.*

blanket *mōfu*

   electric b. *denki-mōfu*

blank paper *hakushi*

blasé *aki-aki shita*

bleach (for hair) *burīchi*

bleach (laundry) *burīchi*

bleeding: I'm b. *Chi ga dete imasu.*

blind (window) *buraindo*

blind (sightless) *mekura*

   color b. *shikimō*

blister *mizubukure*

block (city) *kukaku*

blond *burondo*

blood *chi*

blood pressure *ketsuatsu*

bloodshot eyes *jūketsu shita me*

blouse *burausu*

blowfish *fugu*

blue *aoi*

blunt (of a knife) *kirenai*

board: breadb. *manaita*
 cutting b. *manaita*
 duplicate bridge b. *dyū-purikēto-bōdo*
boarding school *ryōsei no gakkō*
bobby pin *heā-pin*
bobby socks *sokkusu*
body (human) *karada*
body (car) *bodē*
boil (skin infection) *dekimono*
boiled potato *yudeta jagai-mo*
bolt (hardware) *boruto*
bonds (securities) *yūka shō-ken*
bone *hone*
bonnet (child's) *bebī-bō*
Bon Voyage! *Itte irasshai!*
book *hon*
 address b. *jūsho-roku*
 noteb. *nōto*
bookcase *hombako*
book ends *hontate*
book jacket *hon no kabā*
bookkeeper *kaikei*
bookmark *shiori*
bookstore *hon·ya*
bootie (baby shoe) *akambō no kutsu*
boots *nagagutsu*
 riding b. *jōba-gutsu*

 rubber b. *gomu-gutsu*
bored: I'm b. *Taikutsu desu.*
boredom *taikutsu*
born: Where were you b.? *Doko de umaremashita ka?*
borrow: May I b. this? *Kore o karite mo ii desu ka?*
bosom *mune*
boss *bosu*
botanical garden *shokubu-tsuen*
both (persons) *futari-tomo*
both (things) *ryōhō*
bother: Please don't b. *Kekkō desu.*
 What a b.! *Urusai!*
bottle *bin*
 a b. of … *ippon*
 nursing b. *honyūbin*
bottle cap *bin no sen*
bottled beer *binzume-bīru*
bottled gas *puropan-gasu*
bottleneck *nekku*
bottle opener *sen-nuki*
bottom *soko*
 on the b. *soko no hō ni*
Bottoms up! *Kampai!*
bouillon *buiyon*
bourbon *bābon*

bow (of a ship) *senshu*
bow (a salutation) *o-jigi*
bow (knot) *musubime*
bowel movement *daiben*
bowl (for mixing) *bōru*
  a b. of … *ippai*
  salad b. *sarada-bōru*
  soup b. *sūpu-zara*
  sugar b. *satō-ire*
bowlegged *ganimata no*
bowling alley *bōringu-jō*
bowling ball *bōringu-bōru*
box *hako*
  a b. of … *hitohako*
boxer (pugilist) *bokusā*
boxing *bokushingu*
box lunch (sold on RR plat-forms) *ekiben*
box office *kippu-uriba*
boy *otoko no ko*
boy scout *bōi-sukauto*
bracelet *udewa*
braids (hair) *mitsu-ami*
brake *burēki*
  foot b. *futto-burēki*
  hand b. *hando-burēki*
brake rod *burēki-roddo*
branch office *shiten*
branch store *shiten*
brandy *burandē*
brass *shinchū*

brassiere *burajā*
brass polish *shinchū-migaki*
brat (naughty child) *kozō*
brave *yūkan na*
bread *pan*
  a slice of b. *pan hitokire*
  French b. *Furansu-pan*
  fresh b. *atarashii pan*
  loaf of b. *pan ikko*
  raisin b. *budō-pan*
  rye b. *raimugi-pan*
  stale b. *furui pan*
  toasted b. *tōsuto-pan*
  white b. *shiro-pan*
  whole-wheat b. *kuro-pan*
bread & butter *batātsuki-pan*
breadboard *manaita*
bread crumbs *panko*
bread knife *pankiri-naifu*
break: Did it b.? *Kowaremashita ka?*
  How did it b.? *Dō yū fū ni kowaremashita ka?*
breakable *kowareyasui*
breakfast *asa-gohan*
breakfast time *chōshoku-jikan*
breast (woman's) *chibusa*
breath *iki*
  Are you out of b.? *Iki ga*

kireta deshō.

I'm out of b. *Iki ga kiresō ni narimashita.*

Take a deep b. *Fukaku iki o sutte kudasai.*

bride *hanayome*

bridesmaid *hanayome no tsukisoinin*

bridge (card game) *burijji*

bridge (false teeth) *ireba no burijji*

bridge (span) *hashi*

brief (simple) *kantan na*

briefcase *kaban*

bright (intelligent) *kashikoi*

bright (with intense light) *mabushii*

Bring me ..., please. *... o motte kite kudasai.*

Bring me the check, please. *O-kanjō o shite kudasai.*

Bring separate checks, please. *Betsubetsu ni kanjō o shite kudasai.*

British (citizen) *Eikokujin*

British (made in Britain) *Eikoku no*

British Embassy *Eikoku taishikan*

British Isles *Eikoku-shotō*

broccoli *burokkorī*

broken: Is it b.? (damaged) *Kowarete imasu ka?*

Is it b.? (out of order) *Koshō shite imasu ka?*

It's b. (damaged) *Kowarete imasu.*

It's b. (out of order) *Koshō shite imasu.*

broken arm *kossetsu shita ude*

broken leg *kossetsu shita ashi*

bronchitis *kikanshi-en*

bronze *seidō*

brook *kawa*

broom *hōki*

whisk b. *yōfuku-burashi*

brother (his, her, your older) *o-niisan*

(his, her, your younger) *otōtosan*

(my older) *ani*

(my younger) *otōto*

brother-in-law (his, her, your older) *giri-no-o-niisan*

(his, her, your younger) *giri-no-otōtosan*

(my older) *giri-no-ani*

(my younger) *giri-no-otōto*

brown *chairo*
brown sugar *akazatō*
bruise *uchimi*
brunette *burunetto*
brush *burashi*
  clothes b. *yōfuku-burashi*
  hairb. *heā-burashi*
  lipstick b. *benifude*
  shaving b. *hige-sori bura-shi*
  shoeb. *kutsu-burashi*
  toothb. *ha-burashi*
Brussels sprouts *mekyabetsu*
bubble *awa*
bucket *baketsu*
buckle: belt b. *bakkuru*
Buddhism *Bukkyō*
Buddhist (a) *Bukkyōto*
budget *yosan*
buffet (sideboard) *shokki-todana*
buffet (supper) *byuffe*
bug *mushi*
building *tatemono*
  apartment b. *apāto*
  office b. *biru*
bulb: flower b. *kyūkon*
  light b. *denkyū*
bump (a) *kobu*
bumper (car) *bampā*
bunks (double-decker) *ni-*

dan-beddo
bureau (furniture) *tansu*
burglar *dorobō*
burial *maisō*
burn: Don't b. yourself.
  Yakedo shinai yō ni.
burned: I b. myself. *Yakedo shimashita.*
bus *basu*
  sightseeing b. *kankō-basu*
  tour b. *kankō-basu*
bus driver *basu no untenshu*
business: What b. are you in? *O-shigoto wa nan desu ka?*
business card *meishi*
businessman *kaisha-in*
business trip *shutchō*
bus stop *basu-sutoppu*
busy: Are you b.? *Isogashii desu ka?*
  I'm b. *Isogashii desu.*
  I'm not b. *Isogashiku ari-masen.*
butcher *nikuya*
butcher shop *nikuya*
butter *batā*
butter dish *batā-zara*
buttermilk *batā-miruku*
button *botan*
buttonhole *botan ana*

buy: I want to b. .... *o kaitai desu.*
Where can I b. ... ? ...

wa doko de kaemasu ka?
by (near) ... *no soba ni*

C

cab (taxi) *takushī*
cabaret *kyabarē*
cabbage *kyabetsu*
  a head of c. *kyabetsu ikko*
cabin (ship) *kyabin*
cabinet: kitchen c. *shokki-todana*
  medicine c. *kusuri-todana*
cabin number *senshitsu-bangō*
cable (message) *dempō*
caddie *kyadī*
Caesarean *teiō-sekkai*
cake *kēki*
  a slice of c. *kēki hitokire*
  angel c. *enjeru-kēki*
  chocolate c. *chokorēto-kēki*
  decorated c. (W.) *dekorē-shon-kēki*
  sponge c. (J.) *kasutera*
  wedding c. *uedingu-kēki*
  white c. *howaito-kēki*

cake of ice *kōri ikko*
cake of soap *sekken ikko*
cake plate *kēki-zara*
cake powder *kēki-paudā*
cake tin *kēki-gata*
calendar *karendā*
calf (leather) *kiddo*
Call a doctor, please. *O-isha-san o yonde kudasai.*
Call a policeman, please. *O-mawari-san o yonde kudasai.*
Call me a taxi, please. *Takushī o yonde kudasai.*
call: What do you c. this in Japanese? *Kore o Nihongo de nan to iimasu ka?* (*see also* p. 148, General Shopping Phrases)
calm *shizuka na*
camellia *tsubaki*

camera *kamera*
  movie c. *eiga-kamera*
camp (mil.) *kichi*
can (of food, etc.) *kanzume*
  a c. of ... *hitokan*
  empty c. *aki-kan*
can: C. you do it? *Dekimasu ka?*
  I c. do it. *Dekimasu.*
  I can't do it. *Dekimasen.*
  You c. do it. *Anata wa c ekimasu.*
Canada *Kanada*
Canadian (citizen) *Kanada-jin*
Canadian (made in Canada) *Kanada no*
Canadian Embassy *Kanada taishikan*
cancellation *tori-keshi*
cancer *gan*
candelabra *shokudai*
candle *rōsoku*
candlestick *rōsoku-tate*
candy *kyandē*
candy bar *chokorēto*
cane (walking stick) *tsue*
can opener *kan-kiri*
canter (a) *uma no kake-ashi*
cap (headgear) *fuchinashi-bō*
cap: bottle c. *bin no sen*

capsule (pill) *kapuseru*
captain (of a ship) *senchō*
car (automobile) *kuruma*
car (RR) *kyakusha*
caramel *kyarameru*
carbon copy *kābon-kopī*
carbon paper *kābon-shi*
carburetor *kyaburētā*
card: business c. *meishi*
  credit c. *kurejitto-kādo*
  playing c. *torampu*
cardboard box *bōru-bako*
cardigan *kādegan*
car door *kā-doa*
carnation *kānēshon*
carp *koi*
carpenter *daiku*
carpet *jūtan*
carpet sweeper *kāpetto-sōjiki*
carport *shako*
carp streamer *koi-nobori*
car radiator *jidōsha no rajiētā*
car registration *jidōsha-tōroku*
carriage: baby c. *ubaguru-ma*
carrot *ninjin*
carving knife *niku-kiri nai-fu*

carving set *niku-kiri naifu no setto*

cash *genkin*

cashier *suitō-gakari ; kaikei*

casserole (serving dish) *mushiyaki nabe*

cast (for broken bones) *gibusu*

cat *neko*

Catholic (a) *Katorikku*

catsup *kechappu*

cauliflower *karifurawā*

ceiling *tenjō*

celery *serori*

cellar *chikashitsu*

cellophane *serohan*

cement *semento*

cemetery *bochi*

centimeter *senchi* (*see also* p. 171, Liquid and Linear Measures)

cereal: cooked c. *ōto-mīru* dry c. *kōn-furēku*

ceremony *shiki*

Certainly! (I will!) *Kashi-komarimashita!*

Certainly! (That's right!) *Mochiron!*

chafing dish *hotto-purēto*

chains (car) *chēn*

chain store *chēn-sutoā*

chair *isu*

  armc. *hijikake-isu*

  deck c. *dekki-cheā*

  folding c. *oritatami-isu*

  rocking c. *rokkingu-cheā*

  wheelc. *kuruma-isu*

chambermaid *jochū*

champagne *shampen*

chandelier *shanderia*

change (money) *kozeni*

  Do you have c.? *Komakai no ga arimasu ka?*

  Here's your (some) c. *O-tsuri desu.*

  I have c. *Komakai no ga arimasu.*

  I haven't any c. *Komakai no wa arimasen.*

  small c. *komakai kane*

changeable *kawari-yasui*

changed: Have you c. your mind? *O-kangae-nao-shimashita ka?*

  I've c. my mind. *Kangae-naoshimashita.*

change purse *kozeni-ire*

channel (TV) *channeru*

charcoal *sumi*

charge: C. it, please. *Tsuke-te oite kudasai.*

  How much do you c.?

Ikura shimasu ka?
charge account *tsuke*
charming *chāmingu na*
chauffeur *untenshu*
cheap *yasui*
check (bank) *kogitte*
check (amount owed at restaurant or bar) *o-kanjō*
Bring me the c., please. *O-kanjō o shite kudasai.*
checkbook *kogitte-chō*
check-out time *chekku-auto taimu*
checkroom *kurōku*
cheek *hoho*
Cheer up! *Genki o dashi-nasai!*
cheese *chīzu*
cottage c. *katejji-chīzu*
cream c. *kurīmu-chīzu*
macaroni & c. *makaroni-chīzu*
Swiss c. *Suisu-chīzu*
cheese sandwich *chīzu-sandoitchi*
cherry *sakurambo*
cherry blossoms *sakura no hana*
cherry tree *sakura no ki*
chest (furniture) *tansu*

chest (part of the body) *mune*
chewing gum *chūin-gamu*
a pack of c. g. *chūin-gamu hitohako*
chic *shikku na*
chicken (live) *tori*
chicken (meat) *tori-niku*
fried c. *chikin-furai*
roast c. *rōsuto-chikin*
chicken breast *tori no sasa-mi*
chicken leg *tori no ashi*
chicken livers *tori-rebā*
chicken pox *mizu-bōsō*
chicken salad *chikin-sarada*
chicken sandwich *chikin-sandoitchi*
chicken soup *chikin-sūpu*
chicken thigh *tori no momo*
chicken wing *tori no teba*
child *kodomo* (*see also p. 160, Instructions for Child Care*)
childbirth *o-san*
childish *kodomoppoi*
childless couple *ko no nai fūfu*
chilled *hieta*
chills: I have c. *Samuke ga shimasu.*

chilly: It's c. *Samui desu.*
chimney *entotsu*
chin *ago*
china (porcelain) *setomono*
China: mainland C. *Chūgoku*
 Nationalist C. *Taiwan; Chūka Minkoku*
china shop *setomonoya*
Chinatown *Chūka-gai*
chinaware *setomono*
Chinese (citizen) *Chūgoku-jin*
Chinese (made in China) *Chūgoku no*
chip (for gambling) *chippu*
chocolate *chokorēto*
 a bar of c. *chokorēto ichimai*
 hot c. *hotto-kokoa*
chocolate cake *chokorēto-kēki*
chocolate candy *chokorēto*
chocolate ice cream *chokorēto aisu-kurimu*
chocolate milk *chokorēto-miruku*
chocolate pie *chokorēto-pai*
choir *seikatai*
chop (cut of meat) *atsu-giri*

lamb c. *ramu-choppu*
pork c. *pōku-choppu*
veal c. *bīru-choppu*
chopsticks *o-hashi*
chorus *kōrasu*
chorus girl *kōrasu-gāru*
Christian (a) *Kurisuchan*
Christianity *Kirisutokyō*
Christmas *Kurisumasu*
 Merry C.! *Kurisumasu o-medetō!*
Christmas card *Kurisumasu-kādo*
Christmas carol *Kurisumasu-kyaroru*
Christmas Eve *Kurisumasu-ību*
Christmas tree *Kurisumasu-tsurī*
Christmas vacation *Kurisumasu-kyūka*
chrysanthemum *kiku*
church *kyōkai*
cigar *hamaki*
cigarette *tabako*
 a pack of c. *tabako hitoha-ko*
 May I have a c.? *Tabako o itadakemasu ka?*
 Will you have a c.? *Tabako o meshiagarimasu ka?*

cigarette butt *tabako no suigara*

cigarette holder *tabakoyō-paipu*

cigarette lighter *raitā*

cinnamon *shinamon*

circle *maru*

circus *sākasu*

city *toshi*

city office *shiyakusho*

clam *hamaguri*

class: 1st-c. coach *ittōsha*
2nd-c. coach *nitōsha*

clean *kirei na*

cleaner (shop) *kurīninguya*

cleanser (scouring powder) *kurenzā*

cleansing cream *kuren-jingu-kurīmu*

clear (understandable) *aki-raka na*

clear (weather) *hare*

clearing: The weather is c. *Harete kimashita.*

clearly: Speak more c., please. *Motto hakkiri itte kudasai.*

clerk (office) *jimuin*

clerk (shop) *ten·in*

clever *rikō na*

clinic *shinryōjo*

clip: paper c. *kurippu*

clippers (for hedge, etc.) *ueki-basami*

clippers (for nails) *tsume-kiri*

cloakroom *kurōku*

clock *tokei*
alarm c. *mezamashi-dokei*

clogs (wooden) *geta*

cloisonné *shippō-yaki*

close: C. the door (window), please. *Doa (mado) o shimete kudasai.*
What time does it c.? *Nanji ni shimemasu ka?*

close by *sugu chikaku ni*

closed: Is it c.? *Shimatte imasu ka?*
It's c. *Shimatte imasu.*

closet *oshi-ire*

close to ... *no soba ni*

cloth *kire*
a meter of c. *kire ichi-mētoru*
dishc. *fukin*
face c. *tenugui*

clothes (J.) *kimono*

clothes (W.) *yōfuku*
ready-made c. *kisei-fuku*
ready-to-wear c. *bura-sa-gari*

clothes basket *sentakumo-noyō kago*
clothes brush *yōfuku-bura-shi*
clothes dryer *kansōki*
clothes hanger *hangā*
clothesline *monohoshi-tsuna*
   bamboo pole (for drying clothes) *monohoshi-zao*
clothespin *sentaku-basami*
cloud *kumo*
cloudy: It's c. out. *Kumotte imasu.*
clove *chōji*
club (card suit) *kurabu*
clumsy: Don't be c.! *Shikkari shite!*
   I'm c. *Heta desu.*
clutch (car) *kuratchi*
clutch pedal *kuratchi-peda-ru*
coach (RR) *kyakusha*
   1st-class c. *ittōsha*
   2nd-class c. *nitōsha*
coal *sekitan*
   a ton (metric) of c. *sekitan itton*
   charc. *sumi*
coat *kōto*
   fur c. *kegawa no kōto*
   overc. *ōbā*

rainc. *rēnkōto*
suit c. *uwagi*
Coca Cola *koka-kōra*
cockroach *abura-mushi*
cocktail (drink) *kakuteru*
cocktail glass *kakuteru-gurasu*
cocktail party *kakuteru-pātī*
cocktail shaker *shēkā*
cocoa *kokoa*
C.O.D. (cash on delivery) *daikin-hikikae*
coffee *kōhī*
   a cup of c. *kōhī ippai*
   black c. *burakku-kōhī*
   iced c. *aisu-kōhī*
   instant c. *insutanto-kōhī*
coffee cup *kōhī-jawan*
coffee pot *kōhī-potto*
coffee shop *kissa-ten*
coffee table *kōhī-tēburu*
coffin *hitsugi*
cognac *konyakku*
coins: 1-yen c. *ichien-dama*
   5-yen c. *goen-dama*
   10-yen c. *jūen-dama*
   50-yen c. *gojūen-dama*
   100-yen c. *hyakuen-dama*
cold (to the touch) *tsumetai*
   Is it c.? *Tsumetai desu ka?*

It's c. *Tsumetai desu.*

It's not c. *Tsumetaku arimasen.*

cold (weather) *samui*

Is it c. out? *Samui desu ka?*

It's c. out. *Samui desi.*

It's not c. out. *Samuku arimasen.*

cold (temperature) *samui*

Are you c.? *Samui desu ka?*

I'm c. *Samui desu.*

I'm not c. *Samuku arimasen.*

cold (a): Do you have a c.? *Kaze o hikimashita ka?*

I have a c. *Kaze o hikimashita.*

cold cream *kōrudo-kurimu*

cold cuts (lunch meat) *kōrudo-mīto*

cold water *tsumetai o-mizu*

coleslaw *kōrusurō*

collar *eri*

dog c. *inu no kubiwa*

collision *shōtotsu*

color *iro*

color-blind *shikimō*

color film *karā-fuirumu*

color rinse (for the hair) *karā-rinsu*

comb *kushi*

come: Where do you c. from? *O-kuni wa dochira desu ka?*

Come again! *Mata dōzo!*

Come back! *Modotte kinasai!*

Come back soon! *Hayaku kaette irasshai!*

Come down! *Orite kinasai!*

Come here! *Oide nasai!*

Come in! *O-hairi kudasai!*

Come on! (Hurry!) *Sa sa!*

Come quickly! *Hayaku irasshai!*

comedian *komedian*

comedy *kigeki*

comfortable *kokochi-yoi*

Please make yourself c. *Dōzo o-kiraku ni.*

comics *manga*

coming Are you c. (with me)? *Ikimasu ka?*

I'm c. *Ima ikimasu.*

I'm not c. *Ikimasen.*

commanding officer *shikikan*

common (unrefined) *soya na*

common (ordinary) *futsū no*

common-law marriage *dōsei*

common sense *jōshiki*

common stock *kōsai*

compact (for face powder) *kompakuto*

company (business firm) *kaisha*

company (guests) *o-kyaku-san*

concert *konsāto*

concert hall *konsāto-hōru*

condensed milk *kondensu-miruku*

conditioner (for skin or hair) *kondishonā*

conductor (train) *shashō*

cone: ice cream c. *aisu-kurīmu kōn*

Congratulations! *O-medetō gozaimasu!*

conscious: He (she) is c. *Ki ga tsukimashita.*

constipation *bempi*

consul *ryōji*

consulate *ryōjikan*

contagious disease *densem-byō*

conversation *kaiwa*
English c. school *Ei-kaiwa-gakkō*

cook (food preparer) *kokku-san*

cookbook *ryōri no hon*

cooked cereal *ōto-mīru*

cookie *kukkī*

cookie sheet *kukkīyō-rēsu-shi*

cool *suzushii*

copper *dō*

copy (a) *kopī*

cork *koruku*

corkscrew *koruku-nuki*

corn *tōmorokoshi*

corn (callus) *tako*

corned beef *kōn-bīfu*

corner: in the c. *sumi ni*
on the c. *kado ni*
street c. *kado*

corn meal *kōn mīru*   ⌈shi

corn on the cob *tōmoroko-*

cornstarch *kōn-sutāchi*

corporation *kabushiki-gai-sha*

corpse *shitai*

correct *tadashii*

cost: How much does it c.? *Ikura desu ka?*
That c. too much. *Chotto takai desu.*

cottage cheese *katejji-chīzu*

cotton (material) *momen*

absorbent c. *dasshi-men*

cotton thread *momen-ito*

cough *seki*

I have a c. *Seki ga demasu.*

cough drop *sekidome-doroppu*

cough syrup *sekidome-shiroppu*

country (nation) *kuni*

country: in the c. *inaka de*

couple (a married) *fūfu*

couple (several) *futatsu-mit-tsu*

course: Of c.! (That's right!) *Mochiron!*

Of c.! (I will!) *Kashikomarimashita!*

court: tennis c. *tenisu-kōto*

court (of law) *saiban*

courteous *reigi-tadashii*

cousin (his, her, your) *o-itokosan*

(my) *itoko*

cover (lid) *futa*

cover charge *kabā-chāji*

cow *ushi*

coward *·okubyō-mono*

crab *kani*

cracker *kurakkā*

cream *kurīmu*

cold c. *kōrudo-kurīmu*

ice c. *aisu-kurīmu*

whipped c. *hoippu-kurīmu*

cream cheese *kurīmu-chīzu*

cream pitcher *kurīmu-ire*

cream puff *shūkurīmu*

credit *tsuke*

letter of c. *shin·yō-jō*

credit card *kurejitto-kādo*

crib (baby bed) *kodomoyō-betto*

cripple (a) *bikko*

crochet cotton *rēsu-ito*

crochet hook *kagibari*

crooked: It's c. *Magatte imasu.*

crossing (RR) *fumi-kiri*

crosswalk *ōdan-hodō*

crossword puzzle *kurosu-wādo-pazuru*

crowd *hito-gomi*

crowded: It's c. *Konde imasu.*

Will it be c.? *Komu deshō ka?*

crude (person) *yaban na*

crust (pie) *kawa*

crutch *matsuba-zue*

cry: Don't c. *Nakanai de kudasai.*

cucumber *kyūri*

cuff links *kafusu-botan*

cup: a c. of (coffee, etc.) ... *ippai*
   a measuring c. *mejā-kappu*
   a measuring c. of ... *ichi-kappu*
   teac. (J.) *chawan*, (W.) *kō-cha-jawan*
cup & saucer *chawan to uke-zara*
cupboard *shokki-todana*
cup of coffee *kōhī ippai*
cup of tea (J.) *o-cha ippai*, (W.) *kōcha ippai*
curio (antique) *kottōhin*
curious: Aren't you c.? *Kyōmi ga arimasen ka?*
   How c.! *Omoshiroi desu, ne!*
   I'm c. *Kyōmi ga arimasu.*
curry powder *karēko*
curtain (shower) *shawāyō-kāten*

curtain (window) *kāten*
curtain rod *kāten-bō*
curtain rod (grooved for drapes) *kāten-rēru*
cushion *zabuton*
custard *purin*
custard pie *purin-pai*
customer *kyaku*
customs *zeikan*
customs declaration form *zeikan-shinkokusho*
customs duty *kanzei*
customs office *zeikan*
customs officer *zeikanri*
cut: Did you c. yourself? *Doko ka kirimashita ka?*
   Don't c. yourself. *Jibun o kiranai yō ni.*
   I've c. myself here. *Koko o kirimashita.*
cute *kawaii*
cutting board *manaita*

D

daddy *papa*
daily *mainichi no*
daiquiri *daikiri*

daisy *hinagiku*
damp *shimeppoi*
   These are d. *Kore wa*

shimette imasu.
dance (ball) *dansu-pātī*
dancing *dansu*
dandruff *fuke*
Danger! *Abunai!*
dangerous *abunai*
dark *kurai*
dark glasses *kuro-megane*
Darn it! *Shimatta!*
dashboard *dasshubōdo*
date (fruit) *natsume-yashi*
date (engagement) *yakusoku*
date (with boy friend or girl friend) *dēto*
daughter (his, her, your) *o-jōsan*
(my) *musume*
daughter-in-law (his, her, your) *o-yomesan*
(my) *yome*
dawn *hinode*
day *hi*
all d. *ichinichi-jū*
during the d. *nitchū*
every d. *mainichi*
holid. *kyūjitsu*
once a d. *ichinichi ni ichido*
the first d. *saisho no hi*
the last d. *saigo no hi*
the other d. *senjitsu*

the previous d. *mae no hi*
three times a d. *ichinichi ni sando*
twice a d. *ichinichi ni nido*
weekd. *heijitsu* (see also p. 166 for Days of the Week)
day after tomorrow *asatte*
day bed *sofā-beddo*
day before yesterday *oto-toi*
daybreak *yoake*
daydream *musō*
daylight *nikkō*
day nursery *takujisho*
daytime *hiruma*
in the d. *hiruma ni*
dead: He (she) is d. (of one's family) *Shinimashita.*
He (she) is d. (of another family) *Naku narimashita.*
Is he (she) d.? *O-naku nari ni narimashita ka?*
Is it (the animal) d.? *Shinimashita ka?*
dead-end street *fukuro-kōji*
deaf *tsumbo*
deaf & dumb *tsumbo de oshi*

deal (in card game) *fuda o kubaru koto*

dealer (in card game) *dīrā*

December *Jūni-gatsu*

deck (of cards) *torampu hitokumi*

deck (of a ship) *kampan*

deck chair *dekki-cheā*

deep *fukai*

delicious *oishii*
It's d. *Oishii desu.*

deliver: Do you d.? *Todokete kudasaimasu ka?*

delivery boy *haitatsunin*

delivery truck *umpansha*

deluxe *derakkusu*

dent (a) *kubomi*

dentist *haisha-san*

dentist's office *haisha*

denture *ireba*

deodorant (underarm) *asedome*

department store *depāto*

departure time *shuppatsu-jikoku*

dependent (mil.) *gunjin no kazoku*

deposit money (house rental) *shikikin*

desk *tsukue*

dessert *dezāto*

detergent *kona-sekken*

detour *mawarimichi*

dew *tsuyu*

diabetes *tōnyōbyō*

diamond *daiyamondo*

diamond (playing card) *daiya*

diaper *o-mutsu*

diarrhea *geri*

dictionary *jisho*

diet (for health): Are you on a d.? *Genshoku o shite imasu ka?*
I'm on a d. *Genshoku o shite imasu.*

dieting (to lose weight): Are you d.? *Biyōshoku o totte imasu ka?*
I'm d. *Biyōshoku o totte imasu.*
I'm not d. *Biyōshoku o totte imasen.*

difference: It doesn't make any d. *Kamaimasen.*
That makes a d. *Sore nara chigaimasu.*
What's the d.? *Doko ga chigaimasu ka?*

different: It's d. *Chigatte imasu.*

different one *chigau mono*

difficult *muzukashii*
Japanese is very d. *Nihongo wa totemo muzukashii desu.*

dimmer switch (car) *dimā suitchi*

dimple *ekubo*

Diners Club *Dainā Kurabu*

dining car (RR) *shokudōsha*

dining room *shokudō*

dining table *shokutaku*

dinner *bangohan*

dinner party *dīnā-pātī*

dinnertime *yūshoku jikan*

direction *hōkō*

direction signal (car) *hōkō-shijiki*

dirt *doro*

dirty *kitanai*

disagree: I d. *Sō wa omoimasen.*

discard (in bridge) *sute-fuda*

discothèque *diskotekku*

discount *wari-biki*

disease *byōki*

dish (food) *tabemono*

dish (utensil) *o-sara*

dishcloth *fukin*

disheveled *midare-gami no*

dishonest *fushōjiki*

dishpan *arai-oke*

dish rack (for drying) *mizu-kiri*

dish towel *fukin*

dishwasher (electric) *jidō shokki araiki*

disinfectant *shōdokuzai*

disobedient *fujūjun na*

distributor (car part) *disu-toribyūta*

ditch *mizo*

dividend *haitō*

diving board *tobikomi-dai*

divorce *rikon*

divorced: Are they d.? *Karera wa rikon shimashita ka?*

Are you d.? *Anata wa rikon shimashita ka?*

He (she) is d. *Kare (kanojo) wa rikon shimashita.*

I'm d. *Watashi wa rikon shimashita.*

Is he (she) d.? *Kare (kanojo) wa rikon shimashita ka?*

They're d. *Karera wa rikon shimashita.*

We're d. *Watashitachi wa rikon shimashita.*

divorcée *rikon shita hito*

dizzy: Do you feel d.?

Anata wa me ga mawa-rimasu ka?

I feel d. *Me ga mawari-masu.*

do: Can I do it myself? *Watashi ni dekimasu ka?*

Can you do it? *Dekimasu ka?*

Can you do it yourself? *Anata ni dekimasu ka?*

Do it again. *Mō ichido shite kudasai.*

Don't do that! *Ikemasen yo!*

I can do it. *Dekimasu.*

I can do it myself. *Watashi ni dekimasu.*

I can't do it. *Dekimasen.*

I can't do it myself. *Watashi ni wa dekima-sen.*

What am I going to do? *Dō shimashō?*

What are you going to do? *Dō shimasu ka?*

You can do it yourself. *Anata ni wa dekimasu.*

doctor (medical) *o-isha-san*

Call a d., please. *O-isha-san o yonde kudasai. (see*

also p. 155, Health Problems)

doctor's office *i-in*

dog *inu*

dog collar *inu no kubiwa*

dog license *inu no kansatsu*

doing: What are you d.? *Nani o shite imasu ka?*

doll *ningyō*

paper d. *kami-ningyō*

domestic employment agency *kaseifu no sho-kugyō-anteisho*

door: back d. *katte-guchi*

car d. *kā-doa*

Close the d., please. *Doa o shimete kudasai.*

front d. *genkan*

Open the d., please. *Doa o akete kudasai.*

revolving d. *kaiten-doa*

sliding d. *fusuma*

swinging d. *kaiten-doa*

doorbell *yobirin*

door handle (car) *doa-han-doru*

doorknob *doa no totte*

doormat *doa-matto*

doorsill *shiki-i*

doorway *iriguchi*

dose *bunryō*

double *nibai*
double bed *daburu-beddo*
double boiler *daburu-boirā*
double exposure *nijū-utsu-shi*
double room (hotel) *daburu rūmu*
dough (pastry) *neriko*
doughnut *dōnatsu*
down   *shita ni*
   Come d. *Orite kinasai.*
   Put it d. *Sore o okinasai.*
Down? (to elevator operator) *Shita desu ka?*
down payment *atamakin*
downstairs *ikkai*
downtown *hankagai*
dozen (one) *ichi-dāsu*
   half d. *han-dāsu*
draftee *chōhei sareta hito*
drawer (in a chest) *hiki-dashi*
drawing (sketch) *suketchi*
dream *yume*
   dayd. *musō*
drenched: I'm d. *Watashi wa zubunure ni narima-shita.*
dress (J.) *kimono*
dress (W.) *doresu*
   two-piece d. *tsūpīsu*

dressing table *keshōdai*
dressmaker   *doresu-mēkā*
   (see also p. 150, At the Dressmaker or Tailor)
dried fruit *hoshita kudamono*
dried skim milk *kona-miru-ku*
drink: Don't d. it! *Nomanai de!*
   D. it! *Nominasai!*
drinker *sakenomi*
drip-dry (clothing) *nō-airon*
drive: D. carefully, please. *Ki o tsukete hashitte ku-dasai.*
   D. slower (faster), please. *Motto yukkuri (hayaku) hashitte kudasai.*
driver *untenshu*
   bus d. *basu no untenshu*
   chauffeur *untenshu*
   taxi d. *takushi no untenshu*
   truck d. *torakku no unten-shu*
driver's license *unten-men-kyoshō*
driveway *shidō*
drop (of liquid) *hito-shizuku*
drop: Don't d. it! *Otoshite wa ikemasen!*
druggist *kusuriya-san*

drugstore *kusuriya*
drunk (tipsy) *yopparatte imasu*
drunk (a) *yopparai*
dry: Is it d.? *Kawaite imasu ka?*
  It's d. *Kawaite imasu.*
  It's not d. *Kawaite imasen.*
dry (of wine) *karakuchi*
dry cereal *kōn-furēku*
dry cleaner (shop) *kurīninguya*
dry cleaning *dorai-kurīningu*
dryer (for clothes) *kansōki*
dryer (for hair) *heā-doraiyā*
drying rack (for clothes) *monohoshi-kake*
dry shampoo *dorai-shampū*
duck (domesticated) *ahiru*

(wild) *kamo*
  roast d. *rōsuto-dakku*
duck hunting *kamoryō*
dull (blunt) *kirenai*
dull (uninteresting) *tsumaranai*
dumb (stupid) *baka na*
dumb (unable to speak) *oshi no*
dummy (bridge term) *damī*
dump truck *dampu-kā*
duplicate bridge *dyūpurikēto-burijji*
dust *hokori*
duster *hataki*
dusting *o-sōji*
dust mop *yukafuki-moppu*
dustpan *chiri-tori*
duty (tariff) *kanzei*
duty free *menzei*

E

each *ono-ono*
each one *sorezore*
ear *mimi*
earache *jitsū*
  I have an e. *Mimi ga itai*
desu.
early: Am I too e.? *Hayasugimashita ka?*
  I'm e. *Hayaku kimashita.*
  I get up e. in the morning.

Watashi wa asa hayaku okimasu.

It's e. *Hayai desu.*

earmuff *mimi-ōi*

earring *iaringu*

earthquake *jishin*

east *higashi*

Easter *Fukkatsu-sai*

Easter (spring) vacation *haru-yasumi*

Easy! (Take care!) *Ki o tsukete kudasai!*

easy *yasashii*

eating table (J.) *chabudai*

eczema *shisshin*

edge *fuchi*

eel *unagi*

egg *tamago*

  fried e. *tamago-furai*

  hard-boiled e. *katayude-tamago*

  poached e. *otoshi-tamago*

  raw e. *nama-tamago*

  scrambled e. *kaki-tamago*

  soft-boiled e. *hanjuku-ta-mago*

egg beater *awatateki*

eggplant *nasu*

eggs: bacon & e. *bēkon-eggu*

  ham & e. *hamu-eggu*

egg-salad sandwich *tama-go-sarada sandoitchi*

egg white *shiromi*

egg yolk *kimi*

egotistic *rikoshugi na*

eight (items) *yattsu* (see also p. 163, Numbers and Counting)

either one *dochira de mo*

  I don't want e. o. *Do-chira mo irimasen.*

  I'll take e. o. *Dochira de mo ii desu.*

elastic band *gomu-himo*

elbow *hiji*

electric blanket *denki-mōfu*

electric broiler *denki-ryō-riki*

electric dishwasher *jidō shokki araiki*

electric fan *sempūki*

electric heater *dennetsuki*

electric hot plate *denki-konro*

electrician *denkiya*

electricity *denki*

electric light *dentō*

electric mixer (appliance) *mikisā*

electric shaver *denki-ka-misori*

elementary school *shōgak-kō*

elevator *erebētā*

embarrassed: I'm e. *Hazukashii desu.*

    I was e. *Hazukashikatta.*

    Were you e.? *Hazukashikatta no desu ka?*

embassy *taishikan*

emery board *manikyua no kami-yasuri*

employee *jūgyōin*

employer *koyō-nushi*

employment agency *shokugyō anteisho*

empty *kara no*

    Is it e.? *Kara desu ka?*

    It's not e. *Kara de wa arimasen.*

    It's e. *Kara desu.*

Empty it, please. *Sore o kara ni shite kudasai.*

end (the) *owari*

end table (*sofā no*) *waki-tēburu*

enema *kanchō*

energetic: Do you feel e.? *O-genki desu ka?*

    I don't feel very e. *Watashi wa genki de wa arimasen.*

I feel very e. *Watashi wa genki desu.*

engaged (to be married) *kon·yakuchū no*

    Are they e.? *Karera wa kon·yakuchū desu ka?*

    Are you e.? *Kon·yaku shite irasshaimasu ka?*

    I'm e. *Watashi wa kon·yaku shite imasu.*

    I'm not e. *Watashi wa kon·yaku shite imasen.*

    They're e. *Karera wa kon·yaku shite imasu.*

    We're e. *Watashitachi wa kon·yaku shite imasu.*

engagement *kon·yaku*

engagement (date) *yakusoku*

engagement ring *kon·yaku-yubiwa*

engine (car, ship) *enjin*

engine (train) *kikansha*

engine block (car) *enjin-burokku*

engineer *gishi*

engineer (ship) *kikanshi*

engineer (train) *kikanshu*

England *Igirisu*

English: Do you speak E.? *Eigo o hanashimasu ka?*

English-conversation school *Ei-kaiwa-gakkō*
Englishman *Igirisujin*
English teacher *Eigo kyō-shi*
enjoy: E. yourself! *Dōzo o-tanoshimi kudasai!*
enjoyed: I e. it. *Totemo tanoshikatta desu.*
enjoying: Are you e. yourself? *O-tanoshimi desu ka?*
   I'm e. myself. *Totemo tanoshii desu.*
enough *jūbun na*
   Is that e.? *Mō ii desu ka?*
   That's e.! *Mō ii desu!*
   That's e., thank you. *Arigatō gozaimasu. Mō ii desu.*
entrance *iri-guchi*
entrance hall *genkan*
envelope *fūtō*
equal *byōdō na*
eraser *keshi-gomu*
errand *o-tsukai*
escalator *esukarētā*
escape: That was a narrow e. *Yatto tasukarimashita.*
especially *toku ni*
   not e. *betsu ni*

Europe *Yōroppa*
evaporated milk *eba-miru-ku*
even (regular) *kintō na*
evening *yūgata*
   during the e. *yūgata no aida ni*
   Good e.! *Komban wa!*
   in the e. *yūgata ni*
   last e. *sakuban*
   this e. *komban*
   tomorrow e. *ashita no ban*
evening dress *ibuningu*
evening purse *yakaiyō han-do-baggu*
even number *gūsū*
even-tempered *reisei na*
every day *mainichi*
every month *maigetsu*
every morning *mai-asa*
every night *maiban*
every one (people; without exception) *dare demo*
everyone (people or things) *minna*
everyplace *doko demo*
everything *subete*
every time ... *tambi ni*
every week *maishū*
everywhere *doko demo*
every year *mai-nen*

evil *ja-aku*

exaggerated *ōgesa na*

excellent *yūshū na*

excess baggage *chōka-teni-motsu*

exchange rate *kawase-sōba*
  What is the e. r.? *Kawase-sōba wa ikura desu ka?*

excited: Aren't you e.? *Anata wa agatte imasu ka?*
  I'm e. *Agatte imasu.*

excursion *ensoku*

Excuse me! *Gomen nasai!*

exercise (physical) *taisō*

exhausted: I'm e. *Watashi wa kutakuta desu.*

exhaust pipe (car) *haikikan*

exit *deguchi*

expense account *kōsai-hi; hitsuyō keihi*

expensive *takai*

exposure (camera setting) *roshutsu*

exposure (film) *hitokoma*

exposure meter *roshutsu-kei*

express train *kyūkō*

expressway *kōsoku-dōro*

exterminator (man) *shōdo-kuya-san*

extinguisher: fire e. *shōkaki*

extravagant *zeitaku na*

extrovert *gaikōsei no*

eye *me*

eyebrow *mayuge*

eyebrow pencil *mayu-zumi*

eyedropper *megusuri-sashi*

eyeglasses *megane*

eyelash *matsuge*

eyelid *mabuta*

eye liner *ai-rainā*

eye shadow *ai-shadō*

eyesight *shiryoku*

F

face *kao*

face card *efuda*

face cloth *tenugui*

face powder *o-shiroi*

factory *kōjō*

fade: Does this color f.?

*Kono iro wa ochimasu
ka?*

faint: I feel f. *Ki ga tōku
narisō desu.*

fair (equitable) *kōhei na*
That's f. *Sore wa kōhei
desu.*
That's not f. *Fukōhei desu.*

fair (exhibition) *hakuran-
kai*

fairway (golf) *feā-uē*

fall (season) *aki*

fall: Don't f.! *Ochinai yō ni!*

false *nise no*

false eyelashes *tsuke-ma-
tsuge*

false teeth *ireba*

family *kazoku*

famous: a f. man (woman)
yūmei na hito
a f. place *meisho*

fan (folding) *sensu*
electric f. *sempūki*

fan (motor part) *fan*

fan belt (motor part) *fan-
beruto*

far *tōi*
How f. is it? *Dono gurai tōi
desu ka?*
Is it f.? *Tōi desu ka?*

fare (charge) *ryōkin*

half f. *hangaku*
What is the f. to ...?
... made ikura desu ka?

Far East *Kyokutō*

farsighted (eyesight) *enshi*

farther *motto saki*

fashion (style) *fasshon*

fashionable *ryūkō no*

fast: My watch is f. *Watashi
no tokei wa susunde ima-
su.*
This train is f., isn't it?
*Kono kisha wa hayai
desu, ne?*
Your watch is f. *Anata no
tokei wa susunde imasu.*

faster: Drive f., please.
*Motto hayaku hashitte
kudasai.*

fast express train *tokkyū*

fat (grease) *abura*

fat (meat) *abura-mi*

fat (obese) *futotta*

father (his, her, your) *o-
tōsan*
(my) *chichi*

father-in-law (his, her,
your) *giri no o-tōsan*
(my) *giri no chichi*

faucet *jaguchi*

fault: It's my f. *Watashi no*

sekinin desu.

It's not my f. *Watashi no sekinin de wa arimasen.*

It's not your f. *Anata no sekinin de wa arimasen.*

favorite *suki na*

feather duster *hane no hataki*

February *Ni-gatsu*

feeble *kyojaku na*

feeble-minded *seihaku no*

feel: Do you f. better? *Go-kibun wa mō ii desu ka?*

I don't f. good. *Kibun ga warui desu.*

I f. better. *Daibu ii hō desu.*

I f. fine. *Genki desu.*

feeling: Are you f. better? *Go-kibun wa mō ii desu ka?*

How are you f.? *Go-kibun wa ikaga desu ka?*

I'm not f. good. *Kibun ga warui desu.*

I hope you're f. good. *Go-kigen yoroshiku.*

fence *hei*

fender (car) *fendā*

ferryboat (for passengers only) *renrakusen*

(for cars and passengers) *feri-bōto*

festival *o-matsuri*

festivals (Japanese; asterisk denotes legal holiday):

Jan. 1, New Year's Day *O-Shōgatsu**

Jan. 15, Coming-of-Age Day, *Seijin no hi**

Feb. 11, National Foundation Day, *Kenkoku kinembi**

Mar. 3, Girls' Day, *Hina-matsuri*

Mar. 21 or 22, Vernal Equinox Day, *Shumbun no hi**

Apr. 29, Emperor's Birthday, *Tennō-tanjōbi**

May 3, Constitution Day, *Kempō kinembi**

May 5, Children's Day, *Kodomo no hi**

July 7, Star Festival, *Tanabata*

Sept. 15, Respect-for-the-Aged Day, *Keirō no hi**

Sept. 23, Autumnal Equinox Day, *Shūbun no hi**

Oct. 10, Physical Educa-

tion Day, *Taiiku no hi**
Nov. 3, Culture Day, *Bunka no hi**
Nov. 15, 7-, 5-, and 3-Year-Old Children's Day, *Shichi-go-san*
Nov. 23, Labor Thanksgiving Day, *Kinrō kansha no hi** (Note also the New Year's season, which lies anywhere between Dec. 27 and Jan. 7.)

fever *netsu*
Does he (she) have a f.? *Kare (kanojo) wa netsu ga arimasu ka?*
Do you have a f.? *Anata wa netsu ga arimasu ka?*
I don't have a f. *Watashi wa netsu wa arimasen.*
I have a f. *Watashi wa netsu ga arimasu.*
You don't have a f. *Anata wa netsu wa arimasen.*
You have a f. *Anata wa netsu ga arimasu.*

feverish *netsuppoi*
few (a) *futatsu-mittsu*
fiancée *kon·yakusha*
fickle *kimagure na*

field (for grazing cattle) *bokujō*
fig *ichijiku*
file (tool) *yasuri*
nail f. *tsume-yasuri*
filling (for tooth) *jūten*
Fill it up, please. (gas tank) *Mantan ni shite kudasai.*
film (for camera) *fuirumu*
black & white f. *shiro-kuro fuirumu*
color f. *karā-fuirumu*
film (motion picture) *eiga*
filthy (soiled) *kitanai*
final *saigo no*
find Did you f. it? *Mitsukemashita ka?*
find out: I'll f. o. *Kiite mimashō.*
Please f. o. *Kiite mite kudasai.*
fine (small) *komakai*
fine (thin) *usui*
fine: I'm f., thank you. *Genki desu. Arigatō.*
I feel f. *Genki desu.*
That's f.! *Ii desu!*
finger *yubi*
fingernail (*yubi no*) *tsume*
fingernail polish *manikyua;* *nēru porisshu*

fingerprint *shimon*

finished: Have you f.? *Sumimashita ka?*
  I've f. *Mō sumimashita.*
  I haven't f. *Mada sunde imasen.*

fire *hi*

Fire! *Kaji da!*

fire alarm *kasai-hōchi*

fire department *shōbōsho*

fire engine *shōbōsha*

fire exit *hijō-guchi*

fire extinguisher *shōkaki*

fire hydrant *shōkasen*

fire insurance *kasai-hoken*

fireman *shōbōshi*

fireplace *danro*

firescreen *danroyō-sukurīn*

firewood *maki*

fireworks *hanabi*

first (the) *dai-ichi*
  the f. (in a series) *saisho no*
  the f. (of the month) *tsuitachi*

first aid *ōkyū-te-ate*

first-aid kit *ōkyū-te-ate hito-soroi*

first floor *ikkai*

first name *namae*

first time *hajimete*

fish *sakana*

fisherman *ryōshi*

fishhook *tsuri-bari*

fishing rod *tsuri-zao*

fishing tackle *tsuri-dōgu*

fish store *sakanaya*

fish tank (for tropical fish) *sakanayō-tanku*

fit: Does it f.? *Aimasu ka?*
  It doesn't f. *Aimasen.*

fitting (at the dressmaker or tailor) *kari-nui*

five (items) *itsutsu* (see also p. 163, Numbers and Counting)

fix: Can you f. this? *Kore o naosemasu ka?*

flag *hata*

flashlight *kaichū-dentō*

flat (level) *taira na*

flat (apartment) *apāto*

flat tire *panku*

flavor *aji*

flea *nomi*

flea powder *nomitori-ko*

flight number *hikō-bangō*

flimsy *perapera shita*

flint (for lighter) *ishi*

flippers (for skin diving) *furippā*

floor *yuka*

floor (story) *kai*
  basement *chikashitsu*

first f. *ikkai*
ground f. *ikkai*
second f. *nikai*
floor lamp *furoa-sutando*
floor mat (J.) *tatami*
floor waxer *wakkusā*
florist *hanaya*
flour *merikenko*
   a cup (measuring) of f.
   merikenko ichikappu
flour sifter *furui*
flower *hana*
flower arranging *ikebana*
flower bed *kadan*
flower bulb *kyūkon*
flower garden *hanazono*
flower shop *hanaya*
flu *infuruenza*
flush toilet *suisen-benjo*
fly (insect) *hae*
fly swatter *hae-tataki*
fog *kiri*
foggy *kiri-bukai*
   It's f. out. *Soto wa kiri-bukai desu.*
foil: aluminum f. (cooking)
   kukkingu-hoiru
folding chair *oritatami-isu*
folk singer *fōku-shingā*
food *tabemono*
   Chinese f. *Chūka-ryōri*

Japanese f. *Washoku*
Korean f. *Chōsen-ryōri*
Western f. *Yōshoku*
food poisoning *shokuchū-doku*
foot *ashi*
foot brake *futto-burēki*
for (someone) ... *ni*
   Is this f. her (him)? *Kore wa kanojo (kare) ni desu ka?*
   This is f. her (him). *Kore wa kanojo (kare) ni desu.*
   Is this f. me (us)? *Kore wa watashi (watashitachi) ni desu ka?*
   Is this f. them? *Kore wa karera ni desu ka?*
   This is f. me (us). *Kore wa watashi (watashitachi) ni desu.*
   This is f. you. *Kore wa anata ni desu.*
   Will you do it f. me (us)? *Sore o watashi (watashitachi) ni shite kudasaimasu ka?*
forehead *hitai*
foreign *gaikoku no*
foreign country *gaikoku*

foreigner *gaikokujin*

foreign language *gaikokugo*

forest *shinrin*

in the f. *mori no naka*

forget: Don't f! *Wasurenai yō ni!*

I f. *Wasuremashita.*

Forgive me. *Watashi o yurushite kudasai.*

forgot: I f. it. *Sore o wasuremashita.*

I f. something. *Nani ka wasuremashita.*

forgotten: Have you f.? *Wasurete shimaimashita ka?*

I've f. *Wasurete shimaimashita.*

I haven't f. *Wasurete wa imasen.*

fork (eating utensil) *hōku*

formal dress *reifuku*

for sale: Is this f. s.? *Kore wa uri-mono desu ka?*

forty-five r.p.m. record *yonjū-go kaiten*

forward *mae no hō*

found: Have you f. it? *Sore o mitsukemashita ka?*

I f. it. *Mitsukemashita.*

I haven't f. it. *Mitsuke-*

masen deshita.

four (items) *yottsu* (see also p. 163, Numbers and Counting)

fourth: one f. *yombun-no-ichi*

foyer *hōru*

fracture (as of a bone) *hibi*

fragile *koware-yasui*

frame (picture) *gakubuchi*

France *Furansu*

frankfurter *sōsēji*

freckle *sobakasu*

free (of charge): Is it f.? *Tada desu ka?*

It's f. *Tada desu.*

freezer *reitōki*

freighter *kamotsusen*

freight train *kamotsu-ressha*

French (made in France) *Furansu no*

French bread *Furansu pan*

French Embassy *Furansu taishikan*

French fries *poteto-furai*

Frenchman *Furansujin*

French toast *Furenchi-tōsuto*

fresh *shinsen na*

fresh bread *atarashii pan*

fresh-frozen *shinsen-reitō no*

fresh water *shinsen na mizu*

friction tape *zetsuen-tēpu*
Friday *Kin·yōbi*
fried chicken *chikin-furai*
fried egg *medama-yaki*
fried potatoes *poteto-furai*
friend *tomodachi*
frightened: Are you f.? *Kowai desu ka?*
  I'm f. *Kowai desu.*
front (the) *mae*
  in f. of ... *no mae ni*
front door *genkan*
frost *shimo*
frosting (on cake) *aishingu*
frown (a) *shikamettsura*
frozen *reitō no*
frozen foods *reitō-shokuhin*
fruit *kudamono*
  dried f. *hoshita kudamono*
  fresh f. *kudamono*
  stewed f. *nikomi-furūtsu*
fruit & vegetable store *yaoya*
fruit juice *furūtsu-jūsu*
fruit salad *furūtsu-sarada*
frypan *furaipan*
fuel oil *keiyu*
full *ippai ni*
  Is it f.? *Ippai desu ka?*
  It's f. *Ippai desu.*
  It's not f. *Ippai de wa arimasen.*

fun *tanoshimi*
  Have f.! *O-tanoshimi nasai!*
  That was f.! *Yukai deshita, ne!*
funeral service *o-sōshiki*
funny (comical) *okashii*
  How f.! *Okashii!*
funny (strange) *hen na*
  That's f. *Sore wa hen desu.*
fur *kegawa*
fur coat *kegawa-kōto*
fur jacket *kegawa-jaketto*
furnace *boirā*
furnished apartment *kagu-tsuki-apāto*
furnished house *kagutsuki no ie*
furniture *kagu*
furniture polish *kagu no tsuya-dashi*
furniture store *kaguya*
fur piece *kegawa seihin*
fur shop *kegawaya*
fur stole *kegawa no sutōru*
further *sara ni*
fuse (electrical) *hyūzu*
future (the) *mirai*
  in the f. *kore kara*

G

gall bladder *tannō*

game (contest) *shiai*

garage *garēji*

garbage *gomi*

garbage bag *gomi-bukuro*

garbage can *gomi-bako*

garbage collector *gomi-ya-san*

garden *niwa*
  flower g. *hanazono*
  Japanese g. *Nihon tei-en*
  rock g. *sekitei*

gardener *uekiya*

garden hose *mizumaki-hōsu*

garden party *gāden-pātī*

gargle (mouth rinse) *ugai*

Gargle, please. *Ugai o shite kudasai.*

garlic *ninniku*

garlic press *ninniku-tsubushi*

garment *irui*

garment bag *irui-baggu*

gas: I've run out of g.

Gasorin ga kiremashita.

gas (bottled, for cooking) *puropan-gasu*
  a bottle of g. *puropan hitokan*

gas company (selling bottled gas) *gasu-gaisha*

gas meter *gasu-mētā*

gasoline *gasorin*

gas pump *gasorin-pompu*

gas station *gasorin-sutando*

gas-station attendant *sutando-jūgyōin*

gas tank *gasu-tanku*

gate *mon*

gauze mask *masuku*

gear (car) *giyā*

gelatine *zerachin*

general anaesthetic *zenshin-masui*

general delivery (post office) *kyokudome*

generator (car) *jenerētā*

generous *kandai na*

gentleman *shinshi*
genuine *hommono no*
German (citizen) *Doitsujin*
German (made in Germany) *Doitsu no*
German Embassy *Doitsu taishikan*
Germany *Doitsu*
Get out! *Dete ikinasai!*
Get up! *Okinasai!*
gift *okurimono*
gift money (house rental) *reikin*
gin *jin*
ginger *shōga*
girdle *korusetto*
girl *onna no ˈko*
girl (young lady) *o-jōsan*
girl scout *gāru-sukauto*
Give it to me, please. *Watashi ni kudasai.*
Give this to . . . , please. *Kore o . . . -san ni agete kudasai.*
glad *ureshii*
　Aren't you g.? *Ureshii desu ka?*
　I'm g. *Ureshii desu.*
glare *mabushisa*
glass (for drinking) *koppu*
　a g. of . . . *ippai*

beer g. *bīru-gurasu*
cocktail g. *kakuteru-gurasu*
highball g. *haibōru-gurasu*
juice g. *jūsu-gurasu*
martini g. *marutīni-gurasu*
wine g. *wain-gurasu*
glass (material) *garasu*
magnifying g. *kakudaikyō*
glasses (for the eyes) *megane*
bifocals *nishōten-renzu*
dark g. *kuro-megane*
sung. *sangurasu*
glass of milk *miruku ippai*
glass of water *mizu ippai*
glove *tebukuro*
　a pair of g. *tebukuro hito-kumi*
glue *setchakuzai* ⌊*kumi*
go: Let's g.! *Ikimashō!*
　Let's g. back. *Kaerimashō.*
Go away! *Atchi e ikinasai!*
goblet *goburetto*
god *kami*
goggles *chiriyoke-megane*
going: Are you g.? *Anata wa ikimasu ka?*
　Are you g. home? *Anata wa kaerimasu ka?*
　I'm g. *Watashi wa ikimasu.*

I'm g. home. *Watashi wa kaerimasu.*

I'm not g. *Watashi wa ikimasen.*

I'm not g. home. *Watashi wa kaerimasen.*

When are you g.? *Anata wa itsu ikimasu ka?*

gold *kin*
14-kt. g. *jūyon-kin*
18-kt. g. *jūhachi-kin*
white g. *hakkin*
yellow g. *kin*

gold-filled *kimmekki no*

goldfish *kingyo*

golf *gorufu*

golf bag *gorufu-baggu*

golf ball *gorufu-bōru*

golf club *gorufu-kurabu*
a set of g. c. *gorufu-kurabu hitokumi*

golf clubhouse *gorufu-kura-bu*

golf course *gorufu-kōsu*

good *ii*
Is it g.? *Kore wa ii desu ka?*
It's not g. *Yoku nai.*

Good! (I'm happy about it.) *Yokatta desu ne!*

Good! (I understand.) *Yo-roshii!*

Good afternoon! *Konnichi wa!*

Goodbye! (by a family member leaving for a short time) *Itte kimasu!*

Goodbye! (to a family member leaving for a short time) *Itte irasshai!*

Goodbye! (for a long time) *Sayōnara!*

Good evening! *Komban wa!*

Good Friday (Protestant) *Junambi*, (Catholic) *Sei Kin·yōbi*

good idea: That's a g. i. *Sore wa ii kangae desu.*

good-looking (man) *binan-shi*, (woman) *bijo*

good luck *kō-un*

Good luck! *Umaku iku yō ni!*

Good morning! *O-hayō gozaimasu!*

Good night! *O-yasumi na-sai!*

good posture *shisei ga yoi*

good sport *meirō na hito*

good-tempered *yasashii*

good time: Are you having a g. t.? *Ikaga desu ka?*

Did you have a g. t.? *Tanoshikatta desu ka?*

Have a g. t.! *Yukkuri itte irasshai!*

I'm having a g. t. *Tanoshii desu.*

I had a g. t. *Totemo tanoshikatta.*

goose *gachō*

gorgeous *gōka na*

gossip *uwasa*

Go straight ahead. *Massugu itte kudasai.*

government *seifu*

grade (for school work) *seiseki*

gradually *dandan*

gram *guramu*
a g. of ... *ichiguramu no*

grandchild (his, her, your) *o-magosan*
(my) *mago*

grandfather (his, her, your) *o-jiisan*
(my) *sofu*

grandmother (his, her, your) *o-bāsan*
(my) *sobo*

grand slam (bridge) *gurando-suramu*

grandstand *shōmen kan-*

ranseki

grape *budō*

grapefruit *gurēpufurūtsu*

grapefruit juice *gurēpu-furūtsu jūsu*

grape juice *gurēpu-jūsu*

grass *kusa*

grater *oroshi-gane*

grave (burial place) *bochi*

gravel *jari*

gravestone *haka-ishi*

gravy *gurēbī*

gravy boat *gurēbī-ire*

gravy ladle *gurēbī-shakushi*

gray *nezumi-iro*

gray hair *shiraga*

grease (lubricant) *gurīsu*

grease rack (at a service station) *rifuto*

grease spot *abura-jimi*

greasy (of food) *aburakkoi*

great *idai na*

Great Britain *Daiei Teikoku*

green *gurīn*

green (golf) *gurīn*

greenhouse *onshitsu*

green light *midori-shingō*

green peas *gurīn-pīsu*

green pepper *pīman*

groom (newlywed) *hana-muko*

ground (the) *jimen*
ground beef *gyū-hiki-niku*
ground floor *ikkai*
guard (sentry) *hoshō*
guardian *kōkennin*
guess: I g. so. *Sō deshō.*
  I g. not. *Sō ja nai deshō.*
guest *o-kyaku-san*
guest room *kyakuma*
guide (a) *gaido*
  tour g. *ryokō-gaido*

guidebook *ryokō-annai*
gum: chewing g. *chūin-gamu*
gums *haguki*
gun *jū*
  pistol *pisutoru*
  rifle *teppō*
  shotgun *sandanjū*
gutter (road) *mizo*
gutter (roof) *toi*
gynecologist *fujinka*

H

habit (custom) *kuse*
  bad h. *warui kuse*
hail (precipitation) *arare*
hair (on the head) *kami no ke*
  curly h. *makige*
  straight h. *massugu na kami*
hair (body) *ke*
hairbrush *heā-burashi*
haircut *sampatsu*
hairdo *kamigata*
hairdresser *biyōshi*
hair dryer *heā-doraiyā*

hair net *heā-netto*
hairpiece *heā-pīsu*
hairpin *heā-pin*
hair spray *heā-supurē*
half *hambun*
  one h. *hambun*
half an hour *hanjikan*
half fare *hangaku*
half price *hanne*
halfway *chūto*
hallway *rōka*
ham *hamu*
  baked h. *hamu no maru-yaki*

ham & cheese sandwich *hamu-chīzu sandoitchi*

ham & eggs *hamu-eggu*

hamburger (a) *hambāgā*

hamburger meat *hiki-niku*

hammer *hammā*

ham sandwich *hamu-san-doitchi*

ham steak *hamu-sutēki*

hand *te*

by h. *te de*

hand (bridge) *ikkai*

handbag *hando-baggu*

hand brake *hando-burēki*

handful of *hitotsukami no...*

handkerchief *hankachi*

handle *tsumami; totte*

handlebar *jitensha no han-doru*

hand lotion *hando-rōshon*

hand luggage *tenimotsu*

handmade *tesei no*

hand towel *tenugui*

handy: Is it h. (convenient)? *Benri desu ka?*

He's very h. *Kare wa kiyō na hito desu.*

handyman *zatsu-ekifu*

hang: H. it up, please. *Kore o kakete kudasai.*

hanger (for clothes) *hangā*

hangover: Do you have a h.? *Futsuka-yoi desu ka?*

I have a h. *Futsuka-yoi desu.*

happen: How did it h.? *Ittai, dō shita no desu ka?*

When did it h.? *Itsu deshita ka?*

happened: What h.? *Dō shimashita ka?*

happy *shiawase na*

Aren't you h.? *Anata wa tanoshiku arimasen ka?*

Are you h. about it? *Anata wa sore de yokatta no desu ka?*

I'm h. about it. *Watashi wa sore de yokatta no desu.*

I'm very h. *Watashi wa shiawase desu.*

I'm not h. about it. *Watashi wa sore de wa ammari ureshiku arimasen.*

I'm very h. to meet you. *Hajimemashite. Dōzo yoroshiku.*

Happy birthday! *O-tanjōbi o-medetō!*

Happy New Year! *Shinnen o-medetō gozaimasu!*

hard (firm) *katai*

hard (difficult) *muzukashii*

hard-boiled egg *katayude-tamago*

hardware *kanamono*

hardware store *kanamono-ya*

hat *bōshi*

hat shop *bōshiya*

hay fever *kafunshō*

he *kare wa (ga)*

head *atama*

   a h. of lettuce *retasu ikko*

headache: Do you have a h.? *Atama ga itai desu ka?*

   I have a h. *Atama ga itai desu.*

headlight *heddo-raito*

head office *honten*

headwaiter *chifu-uētā*

healthy *kenkō na (see also p. 155, Health Problems)*

hear: Can you h. me? *Kikoemasu ka?*

   Do you h. that? *Are ga kikoemasu ka?*

   I can't h. you. *Kikoemasen.*

   I don't h. it. *Kikoemasen.*

   I h. it. *Kikoemasu.*

hearing aid *hochōki*

hearse *reikyūsha*

heart *shinzō*

heart (card) *hāto*

heart attack *shinzō-mahi*

heart trouble *shinzōbyō*

heat *netsu*

heat (climate) *atsusa*

heater (car) *hītā*

heater (electric) *dennetsuki*

heating pad (electric) *denki-anka*

heat resistant *tai-netsusei no*

heat wave *nekki*

heavy *omoi*

hedge *ikegaki*

hedge clippers *ueki-basami*

heel (of the foot) *kakato*

heel (of a shoe) *hīru*

   high h. *hai-hīru*

   low h. *rō-hīru*

helicopter *herikoputā*

Hello! *Konnichi wa!*

Hello. (on the telephone) *Moshi, moshi.*

Help! *Tasukete!*

help: Can you h. me, please? *Tasukete kuda-saimasen ka?*

helped: It can't be h.

Shikata ga nai.

helpful: You've been very h. (to someone who has served in the course of duty) *Go-kurō-sama.*

You've been very h. (to someone who has gone out of his way) *O-sewa-sama deshita.*

hem *fuchi*

H. this for me, please. *Suso o kagatte kudasai.*

hemorrhage *shukketsu*

hemorrhoids *ji*

her *kanojo o*

for (to) h. *kanojo ni (see also hers)*

her (belonging to) *kanojo no*

herbs *yakusō*

Here (is something for you)! *Dōzo!*

here *koko*

over h. *kochira*

Turn h. *Koko o magatte kudasai.*

Here he (she, it) comes. *Kimashita.*

Here he (she) is. *Kare (kanojo) ga koko ni imasu.*

_____ *Koko ni imasu.*

Here it is. *Koko desu.*

Here's my name and address. *Kore wa watashi no namae to jūsho desu.*

Here they (people) are. *Karera ga koko ni imasu.*

Here they come. *Kimashita.*

Here we are. *Watashitachi ga koko ni imasu.*

Here you are. (This is for you.) *Hai, dōzo.*

herring *nishin*

hers: Is it h.? *Kanojo no desu ka?*

It's h. *Kanojo no desu.*

It's not h. *Kanojo no de wa arimasen.*

hiccups *shakkuri*

I have the h. *Shakkuri ga demasu.*

high *takai*

high (drunk) *chidori-ashi no*

highball *haibōru*

highball glass *haibōru-gura-su*

high beam (headlight) *uwa-muki-raito*

high-priced *takai*

high school *kōkō*

high-strung *ki no hatta*

high tide *manchō*
highway *haiuē*
hill *oka*
him *kare o*
  for (to) h. *kare ni*
hip *koshi*
his *kare no*
  Is it h.? *Kare no desu ka?*
  It's h. *Kare no desu.*
  It's not h. *Kare no de wa*
    arimasen.
hoarse *shagare-goe*
hobby *shumi*
hole *ana*
hole in one *hōru-in-wan*
holiday *kyūjitsu*
holidays (see festivals)
hollow *garandō na*
home *uchi*
  Is Mrs. ... h.? *... fujin wa*
    go-zaitaku desu ka?
  Mrs. ... is h. ... *fujin wa*
    go-zaitaku desu.
  Mrs. ... is not h. ... *fujin*
    wa o-rusu desu.
home economics *kaseigaku*
home life *katei-seikatsu*
homely (plain) *shisso na*
homesick: Are you h.?
  Hōmushikku desu ka? I'm
  h. *Hōmushikku desu.*

  I'm not h. *Hōmushikku de*
  wa arimasen.
  I hope you're not h.
    Anata ga hōmushikku de
    nai to ii desu ga.
homework (school) *shuku-*
  dai
honest *shōjiki na*
honey *hachimitsu*
honeymoon *shinkon-ryokō*
hood (car) *bonnetto*
hook (for hanging) *kagi*
hook: crochet h. *kagibari*
  fishh. *tsuribari*
hook & eye *hokku*
hope: I h. not. *Sō de nai to*
  ii desu, ne.
  I h. so. *Sō da to ii desu,*
  ne.
horizontal *suihei no*
horn (car) *kurakushon*
hors d'oeuvres *ōdoburu*
horse *uma*
horseback riding *jōba*
horse race *keiba*
horse show *hōsu-shō*
hose *hōsu*
  garden h. *mizumaki-hōsu*
hospital *byōin* (see also
  p.155, Health Problems)
hospital insurance *kenkō*

   hoken

host *shujin*

hostess *onna-shujin*
   bar h. *bā no hosutesu*

hot (to the touch) *atsui*
   Is it h.? *Atsui desu ka?*
   It's h. *Atsui desu.*
   It's not h. *Atsuku arima-sen.*

hot (with seasoning) *karai*

hot (weather and body temperature) *atsui*
   Are you h.? *Atsui desu ka?*
   I'm h. *Atsui desu.*
   Is it h. out? *Soto wa atsui desu ka?*
   It's h. out. *Atsui desu.*
   It's not h. out. *Atsuku ari-masen.*

hot cake *hotto-kēki*

hot chocolate *hotto-kokoa*

hot dog (frankfurter) *hotto-doggu*

hotel (J. style) *ryokan*, (W. style) *hoteru*

hot plate (electric) *denki-konro*

hot spring *onsen*

hot-springs resort *onsen*

hot towel *o-shibori*

hot water *o-yu*, (for drinking) *sayu*

hot-water bottle (J., metal) *yutampo*, (W., rubber) *hotto-uōtā-botoru*

hot-water heater *suchīmu*

hour (an) *ichijikan*
   an h. ago *ichijikan mae*
   an h. from now *ichijikan saki*

house *ie*

housebroken cat (dog) *oku-nai de katte iru neko (inu)*

housecoat *heyagi*

housekeeper *kaseifu* (see also p. 158, Housekeeping Instructions)

housewarming (party) *hik-koshi-iwai*

How? *Dō shite?*

How are you? *Ikaga desu ka?*

How are you feeling? *Go-kibun wa ikaga desu ka?*

How did it break? *Dō yū fū ni kowaremashita ka?*

How did it happen? *Ittai dō shita no desu ka?*

How do you do? (at formal

presentation) *Hajime-mashite. Dōzo yoroshiku.*

How do you do? (Hello!) (in the morning) *O-hayō gozaimasu!* (during the day), *Konnichi wa!* (in the evening) *Komban wa!*

How do you say that in Japanese? *Sore wa Nihongo de nan to iimasu ka?*

How early is it? *Dono gurai hayai desu ka?*

How far is it? *Dono gurai tōi desu ka?*

How late is it? *Dono gurai osoi desu ka?*

How long is it? *Dono gurai nagai desu ka?*

How long will it take? *Dono gurai kakarimasu ka?*

How many (people) **are there?** *Nannin gurai imasu ka?*

How many (things) **are there?** *Ikutsu arimasu ka?*

How much does it cost? *Ikura desu ka?*

How much do you charge? *Ikura shimasu ka?*

How much is it? *Ikura desu ka?*

How much is left? *Dono gurai nokotte imasu ka?*

How old are you? *O-ikutsu desu ka?*

How old is it? *Dono gurai furui desu ka?*

How short is it? *Dono gurai mijikai desu ka?*

How soon can you do it? *Dono gurai hayaku dekimasu ka?*

How soon will it be? *Itsu ni narimasu ka?*

hub cap *habu-kyappu*

huge *kyodai na*

human being *ningen*

humid *shikke no ōi*
It's h. *Mushiatsui desu.*

hundred (one) *hyaku*

hungry: Are you h.? *O-naka ga sukimashita ka?*
I'm h. *O-naka ga sukimashita.*
I'm not h. *O-naka wa suite imasen.*

hunting license *shuryō-*

kansatsushō
hurry: Are you in a h.?
Isoide imasu ka?
Don't h. *Isogazu ni yatte
kudasai.*
I'm in a h. *Isoide imasu.*
I'm not in a h. *Isoide
imasen.*
Hurry, please! *Isoide kudasai!*
hurt: Does it h.? *Itai desu
ka?*

Don't h. yourself. *Kega o
shinai yō ni.*
It doesn't h. *Itaku arimasen.*
It h. *Itai desu.*
husband (her, your) *go-
shujin*
(my) *shujin*
hydrofoil *suichūyokusen*
hypochondriac *yū-utsushō
kanja*
hypodermic *hika-chūshaki*

I *watashi wa (ga)*
ice *kōri*
ice cream *aisu-kurīmu*
chocolate i. c. *chokorēto
aisu-kurīmu*
vanilla i. c. *banira aisu-
kurīmu*
ice cream cone *aisukurīmu
kōn*
ice cream soda *aisu-kurīmu
sōda*
ice cream sundae *kurīmu-
sandē*

ice cube *aisu-kyūbu*
iced *hiyashita*
iced coffee *aisu-kōhī*
iced tea *aisu-tī*
ice skates *aisu-sukēto*
ice water *aisu-uōtā*
icicle *tsurara*
icing (on cake) *aishingu*
idea: That's a good i. *Sore
wa ii kangae desu.*
identification card *mibun-
shōmeisho*
ignition (car) *sutāta-suitchi*

ignorant *muchi na*
ill *byōki*
  Are you i.? *Byōki desu ka?*
  He (she) is i. *Kare (kanojo) wa byōki desu.*
  I'm i. *Byōki desu.*
illegitimate child *shiseiji*
illness *byōki*
illustration *zu*
imitation *magai*
immature *mijuku na*
immediately *sugu ni*
Immigration Office *Nyūkoku kanri-kyoku*
immoral *fudōtoku na*
impatient *tanki na*
  Don't be i.! *Ochitsuite kudasai!*
impolite *shitsurei na*
important *jūyō na*
impossible *fukanō na*
  That's i. *Sore wa fukanō desu.*
inaccurate *fuseikaku na*
in a line *ichiretsu ni*
in & out *detari haittari*
incense *kō*
incense burner *kōro*
including bath & toilet *basu-toire-tsuki*
including bath & meal *ni-shoku-tsuki*
income *shūnyū*
income tax *shotokuzei*
income tax return *shotoku-zei-shinkokusho*
inconvenient *fuben na*
incorrect *fuseikaku na*
India *Indo*
indigestion *shōka furyō*
  I have i. *O-naka o kowashimashita.*
inexpensive *yasui*
infection *kansen*
inferior *ototta*
inferiority complex *rettōkan*
information *tsūchi*
information desk *annaijō*
  Where is the i. d.? *Annaijō wa doko desu ka?*
injection *chūsha*
injured *kega o shita*
ink (J.) *sumi*
ink (W.) *inki*
inn (J.) *ryokan*
inner tube *chūbu*
insane *kichigai*
insect *mushi*
insect repellent *mushi-yoke*
inside ... *no uchigawa ni*
inside (indoors) *naka*

inside out *ura-gaeshi*
inspection (of car) *shaken*
installment (payment) *bun-katsukin*
installment plan (credit buying) *geppu*
instant coffee *insutanto-kōhī*
instead of ... *no kawari ni*
instep (of a shoe) *kutsu no kō*
instep (of foot) *ashi no kō*
insurance *hoken*
  car i. *jidōsha-hoken*
  fire i. *kasai-hoken*
  hospital i. *kenkō-hoken*
  life i. *seimei-hoken*
  theft i. *tōnan-hoken*
  unemployment i. *shitsu-gyō-hoken*
insurance policy *hoken-shōken*
intelligent *richiteki na*
interchangeable: They're i. *Okikaeraremasu.*
interest (money) *rishi*
interested: Are you i.? *Kyōmi ga arimasu ka?* I'm i. *Kyōmi ga arimasu.* I'm not i. *Kyōmi wa arimasen.*

interesting: He (she) is i. *Omoshiroi hito desu.* That's i. *Sore wa omoshiroi desu.*
intermission (at a concert) *kyūkei*, (at the theater) *makuai*
intern *intān*
interpreter *tsūyaku*
interruption *jama*
intestine *chō*
introduce: May I i. you to Mr. ... ? ... *-san o go-shōkai itashimasu.*
introvert *naikōsei no*
invalid *byōnin*
invitation *shōtai*
iodine *yōdochinki*
IOU *shakuyōsho*
iris *ayame; hana-shōbu*
iron (metal) *tetsu*
iron (for pressing) *airon*
  steam i. *jōki-airon*
ironing board *airon-dai*
itch: I have an i. *Kayui desu.*
itches: It i. *Kayui desu.*
itinerary *ryotei*
ivory *zōge*
ivy *tsuta*

J

jack (for car) *jakki*
jack (playing card) *jakku*
jacket: book j. *hon-kabā*
  fur j. *kegawa-jaketto*
  sports j. *supōtsu-jaketto*
jade *hisui*
jail *keimusho*
January *Ichi-gatsu*
Japan *Nihon*
Japan Air Lines (JAL) *Nihon Kōkū*
Japanese (citizen) *Nihonjin*
Japanese (made in Japan) *Nihon no*
Japanese (language) *Nihongo*
  How do you say that in J.? *Sore wa Nihongo de nan to iimasu ka?*
  What is this called in J.? *Kore wa Nihongo de nan to iimasu ka?*
Japanese food *Washoku*
Japan National Railways

(JNR) *Kokutetsu*
Japan Travel Bureau (JTB) *Nihon Kōtsū Kōsha*
jar *tsubo*
  a j. of ... *hitobin*
jaw *ago*
jeans (dungarees) *jiipan*
jeep *jīpu*
jello *zerī*
jelly *zerī*
jellyfish *kurage*
jelly sandwich *zerī-sando-itchi*
Jesus Christ (Protestant pronunciation), *Iesu Kirisuto*, (Catholic pronunciation) *Iezusu Kirisutosu*
jet plane *jettoki*
jewelry *hōseki*
jewelry box *hōseki-bako*
jewelry shop *hōseki-ten*
jigger (drink measure) *jigā*
jigsaw puzzle *hame-e*

job *shokugyō*
jockey *keiba no kishu*
jockstrap *sapōtā*
joke *jōdan*
  practical j. *waru-fuzake*
  risqué j. *waidan*
joker (card) *jōkā*
journey *ryokō*
judge (in court of law) *sai-bankan*
juice *jūsu*
  apple j. *appuru-jūsu*
  fruit j. *furūtsu-jūsu*
  grape j. *gurēpu-jūsu*

  grapefruit j. *gurēpufurūtsu-jūsu*
  orange j. *orenji-jūsu*
  pineapple j. *pain-jūsu*
  prune j. *puramu-jūsu*
  tomato j. *tomato-jūsu*
juice glass *jūsu-gurasu*
jukebox *jūku-bokkusu*
July *Shichi-gatsu*
jump rope *nawa-tobi*
June *Roku-gatsu*
junk shop *kuzuya*
juvenile delinquent *furyō shōnen*

K

Keep this. *Kore o totte oite kudasai.*
kennel *inugoya*
kerosene *sekiyu*
ketchup *kechappu*
kettle: teakettle *yakan*
key *kagi*
key (car) *kī*
key ring *kī-horudā*
kid (child) *kodomo*
kilogram *kiro (guramu)*

  a k. of … *ichikiro* (see also p. 171, Liquid and Linear Measures)
kilometer *kiro (mētoru)* (see also p. 172, Speed Table)
kind (polite) *shinsetsu na*
kind: What k. is it? *Donna no desu ka?*
kindergarten *yōchien*
kindling wood *takigi*
king (playing card) *kingu*

kiss *kisu*
kitchen *daidokoro*
kitchen cabinet *shokki-to-dana*
kitchen sink *nagashi*
kitchen stove *gasu-renji*
kitchen table *kichin-tēburu*
kitchen towel *kichin-taoru*
kitchenware *daidokoro-yō-hin*
kite *tako*
kitten *koneko*
kleenex *tisshu pēpā*
knee *hiza*
knife *naifu*

bread k. *pan-kiri naifu*
carving k. *niku-kiri naifu*
kitchen k. *hōchō*
paring k. *kawa-muki hōchō*
knife sharpener *hōchō-togi*
knit suit *nitto-sūtsu*
knitting *amimono*
knitting needle *amibō*
knitwear *nitto-ueā*
knob *totte*
knot *musubi-me*
Korea: North K. *Kita-chōsen*
    South K. *Kankoku*
Korean (citizen) *Kankokujin*

L

label *fuda*
labor pains *jintsū*
lace *rēsu*
lacquer ware *shikki*
ladder *hashigo*
ladies' room *keshōshitsu*
    Where's the l. r.? *Keshō-shitsu wa doko desu ka?*
ladle *shakushi*
    gravy l. *gurēbi-shakushi*

lady *fujin*
    young l. (unmarried) *o-jō-san*
lake *mizu-umi*
lamb (meat) *ramu*
lamb chop *ramu-choppu*
lamb leg (cut of meat) *ramu-reggu*
lamb stew *ramu-shichū*
lame *bikko*

lamp *sutando*
  floor l. *furoa-sutando*
  sun l. *taiyōtō*
  table l. *takujō-sutando*
lampshade *sutando no kasa*
landing (airplane) *chakuriku*
landlady *yanushi no okusan*
landlord *yanushi ; ōya-san*
language *kotoba*
lantern (J., metal) *tōrō*, (J.,
  paper) *chōchin*, (J.,
  stone) *ishi-dōrō*
lap *hiza*
lapel *eri no ori-kaeshi*
lard *rādo*
large *ōkii*
laryngitis *kōtōen*
last (the) *saigo no*
  next to l. *saigo kara nibamme*
last evening *sakuban*
last month *sengetsu*
last name *myōji*
last night *sakuban*
last time *kono mae*
last week *senshū*
last year *kyonen*
late *osoi*
  Am I l.? *Osoi desu ka?*
  Don't be l.! *Osoku naranai
  vō ni!*

  I'm l. *Osoku narimashita.*
  Is it l.? *Osoi desu ka?*
  It's l. *Osoi desu.*
lately *konogoro*
later *ato de*
  I'll see you l. *Mata ato de.*
Later! *Nochi hodo !*
latest style: It's the l. s.
  Ryūkō desu.
laundress *sentaku-onna*
laundry *sentaku-mono*
laundry (commercial) *sen-
  takuya*
lavatory *toire*
lawful *gōhō no*
lawn *shibafu*
lawn mower *shiba-kariki*
lawyer *bengoshi*
laxative *gezai*
lazy *namake-mono*
lead (metal) *namari*
leaf *ha*
leak *more-guchi*
lean meat *akami no niku*
leap year *urū-doshi*
lease *shakuyō-kigen*
leash *kawahimo*
leather *kawa*
  alligator *wanigawa*
  calfskin *kiddo*
  patent l. *enameru-gawa*

pigskin *butagawa*
snakeskin *hebigawa*
leather goods *kawa-seihin*
leave: Don't l. *Itte wa ikemasen.*
  What time does it l.? *Nanji ni shuppatsu shimasu ka?*
leaving: Are you l.? *Mō o-kaeri desu ka?*
  I'm l. *Kaerimasu.*
  I'm not l. *Dekakemasen.*
  I must be l. now. *Mō o-itoma itashimashō.*
  What time are you l.? *Nanji ni shuppatsu shimasu ka?*
lecture *kōen*
left (opp. of right) *hidari*
  on the l. side *hidarigawa ni*
  Turn l. *Hidari e magatte kudasai.*
left-handed *hidari-kiki no*
leftovers (food) *nokori-mono*
left side *hidari no hō*
leg *ashi*
legal *hōritsujō no*
leg of lamb *ramu-reggu*
leisure *rejā*
leisure time *hima*

lemon *remon*
lemonade *remonēdo*
lemon pie *remon-pai*
lemon squeezer *remon-shibori*
Lend me …, please. *… o kashite kudasai.*
Lengthen this, please. *Kore o nagaku shite kudasai.*
Lent *Shijunsetsu*
less *yori sukunai*
  more or l. *tashō*
letter (epistle) *tegami*
  love l. *rabu-retā*
  registered l. *kakitome*
  special-delivery l. *sokutatsu*
letter (character) *moji*
letter of credit *shin·yō-jō*
letter opener *pēpā-naifu*
lettuce *retasu*
  a head of l. *retasu ikko*
level *taira na*
level-headed *reisei na*
liar *uso-tsuki*
librarian *toshokan-in*
library *toshokan*
license: dog l. *inu no kansatsu*
  driver's l. *unten menkyo-shō*

hunting l. *shuryō kansa-tsushō*

license plate *nambā-purēto*

lid (cover) *futa*

lie (falsehood) *uso*

lifeboat *kyūmeitei*

lifeguard *kyūjo-in*

life insurance *seimei-hoken*

life jacket *kyūmeigu*

life preserver *kyūmei-buku-ro*

light (artificial) *akari*

  traffic l. *kōtsū-shingō*

  Turn off the l., please. *Denki o keshite kudasai.*

  Turn on the l., please. *Denki o tsukete kudasai.*

light (natural) *hikari*

light (weight) *karui*

light bulb *denkyū*

lighter: cigarette l. *raitā*

lighter flint *raitā-ishi*

lighter fluid *raitā-oiru*

lighter gas *raitā-gasu*

light meter *roshutsukei*

lightning *kaminari*

light switch *denki no suitchi*

like: Do you l. it? *O-suki desu ka?*

  I don't l. it. *Suki de wa arimasen.*

  I l. it. *Suki desu.*

  I l. it very much. *Dai-suki desu.*

lilac *rairakku*

limp *bikko*

line (queue) *retsu*

  in a l. *ichiretsu ni*

linen (bed & table) *shītsu to tēburu-kurosu*

lingerie *ranjerī*

liniment *nuri-gusuri*

lining *ura*

linoleum *rinoryūmu*

lips *kuchibiru*

lipstick *kuchibeni*

lipstick brush *benifude*

liquid *ekitai*

liquor (J.) *sake*, (W.) *yōshu*

liquor store *sakaya*

list (of items) *mokuroku*

list (of people) *meibo*

Listen! *Kikinasai!*

listening: Are you l.? *Kiite imasu ka?*

  I'm l. *Kiite imasu.*

liter *rittoru*

  a l. of ... *ichirittoru* (see also p. 171, Liquid and Linear Measures)

little *chiisai*

  too l. *chiisa-sugimasu*

little (a) *sukoshi*
  a l. more, *mō sukoshi*
  a l. less *motto sukunaku*
little by little *dandan*
live: I l. at .... *ni sunde imasu.*
  Where do you l.? *Doko ni sunde irasshaimasu ka?*
lively *genki na*
liver: beef l. *gyū-rebā*
  chicken l. *tori-rebā*
liver (human) *kanzō*
living room *kyakuma*
loafers (shoes) *mokashin*
loaf of bread *pan ikko*
loan (a) *shakkin*
lobster *ise-ebi*
local anaesthetic *kyokusho-masui*
local train *futsū-ressha*
lock (a) *kagi*
logs (for fireplace) *maruta*
lollipop *bōtsuki-ame*
lonely *sabishii*
long (in time) *nagai aida*
  Don't be l. *Hayaku kaette kite kudasai.*
  How l. will it take? *Dono gurai kakarimasu ka?*
  It's been a l. time (since I saw you). *Shibaraku*

deshita, ne.
long (length) *nagai*
  How l. is it? *Dono gurai nagai desu ka?*
  It's too l. *Sore wa naga-sugimasu.*
long-distance call *chōkyo-ri-denwa*
long-distance operator *chōkyori-denwa kōkan-shu*
long-playing record *erupī-rekōdo*
long-waisted *dōnaga no*
Look! *Goran nasai!*
  Don't l. *Mite wa ikemasen.*
Look out! *Abunai!*
loose *yurui*
loose powder *kona-oshiroi*
Lord's Prayer *Shu no Inori*
lose: Don't l. it. *Nakushite wa ikemasen.*
lost: I'm l. (disoriented) *Michi ni mayotte imasu.*
lost & found office *ishi-tsubutsu-atsukaijo*
lost article *wasure-mono*
lot (plot of land) *shikichi*
lot: a l. *takusan*
lotion *rōshon*
lottery *kuji-biki*

hand l. *hando-rōshon*

eye l. *megusuri*

lotus *hasu no hana*

loud: It's too l. (of a radio or TV) *Oto ga ōki-sugima-su.*

You're too l.! (to a child) *Yakamashii desu, yo!*

love *ai*

love affair *jōji*

love at first sight *hitome-bore*

love letter *rabu-retā*

lovely *utsukushii*

love marriage *ren·ai-kek-kon*

love song *koi no uta*

low *hikui*

low beam (headlight) *shi-tamuki-raito*

low-cut *rōkatto*

lower berth *gedan*

low-priced *yasui*

low tide *kanchō*

lubricate: Please l. the car. *Gurisu-appu shite kuda-sai. (see also ,p. 151, At the Service Station)*

lubricating oil *junkatsuyu*

lubrication *chūyu*

luck: bad l. *aku-un*

good l. *kō-un*

Good l.! *Umaku iku yō ni!*

lucky: I'm l. *Watashi wa un ga ii desu.*

You're l. *Un ga yokatta no desu, ne.*

lucky break *un ga ii koto*

luggage *nimotsu*

hand l. *tenimotsu*

lukewarm water *nurumayu*

lump (swelling) *kobu*

lunch *o-hirugohan*

box l. (sold on RR plat-forms) *ekiben*

luncheon (party) *tī-pātī*

lunch meat (cold cuts) *kōrudo-mīto*

lunchtime *o-hiru*

lung *hai*

luxurious *zeitaku na*

M

macaroni *makaroni*

macaroni & cheese *makaroni-chīzu*

machine *kikai*

mad (angry) *okotta*

made-to-order *chūmon-atsurae*

magazine *zasshi*

magnifying glass *kakudai-kyō*

magnifying mirror *kakudaikyō*

mahogany *mahoganī*

   Philippine m. *(lauan) rawan*

maid (servant) *mēdo* (*see also* p. 157, Interviewing a Maid)

mail *yūbin* (*see also* p. 162, At the Post Office

mailbox (receiving) *yūbin-uke,* (sending) *posuto*

mailman *yubin·ya-san*

mail order *tsūshin-hambai*

makeup *keshō*

man *otoko no hito*

   young m. (unmarried) *seinen*

manager *shihainin*

Manhattan (cocktail) *Manhattan*

manicure *manikyua*

manicure scissors *manikyua-basami*

manicurist *manikyua-shi*

manufacturer *mēkā*

many *takusan no*

   How m. (people) are there? *Nannin gurai imasu ka?*

   How m. (things) are there? *Ikutsu arimasu ka?*

   too m. *amari takusan*

many more *motto takusan*

map *chizu*

   road m. *dōro-chizu*

maraschino cherry *marasukino-cherī*

March *San-gatsu*

margarine *māgarin*
marine (a) *kaigun-hei*
marine (of the sea) *umi no*
marjoram *mayorana*
marked-down *ne-biki*
market *ichiba*
marmalade *mamarēdo*
marriage: arranged m. *mi-ai-kekkon*
 love m. *ren·ai-kekkon*
married *kekkon shita*
  Are you m.? *Anata wa kekkon shite imasu ka?*
  He (she) is m. *Kare (kanojo) wa kekkon shite imasu.*
  I'm m. *Watashi wa kekkon shite imasu.*
  I'm not m. *Watashi wa kekkon shite imasen.*
  Is he (she) m.? *Kare (kanojo) wa kekkon shite imasu ka?*
marshmallow *mashumaro*
martini *marutīni*
martini glass *marutīni-gurasu*
mascara *masukara*
mashed potatoes *masshu-poteto*
mask *o-men*

masking tape *hōsōyō tēpu*
mason *sakan·ya*
mass (rite) *misa*
massage (J.) *amma-jutsu*
massage (W.) *massāji*
masseur *otoko-amma*
masseuse *onna-amma*
master (of the house, employer, etc.) *shujin*
masterpiece *kessaku*
mat: floor m. (J.) *tatami*
 place m. *tēburu-matto*
match *matchi*
match: sports m. *shiai*
matchbox *matchi-bako*
material (cloth) *kiji*
matter: It doesn't m. *Ka-maimasen.*
  Something's the m. *Nani ka arimashita, ne.*
  What's the m.? *Dō shimashita ka?*
mattress *mattoresu*
 air m. *eā-mattoresu*
mature *seijuku shita*
maximum *saidaigen*
May *Go-gatsu*
maybe *tabun*
May I borrow this? *Kore o haishaku shite ii desu ka?*

May I see that? *Sore o misete itadakemasu ka?*

May I take this? *Kore o itadakemasu ka?*

May I use the telephone? *Denwa o kashite kudasai.*

May I use this? *Kore o tsukatte mo ii desu ka?*

mayonnaise *mayonēzu*

mayor (of a city) *shichō*

me *watashi o*
  for (to) m. *watashi ni*

meadow *nohara*

meal (repast) *shokuji*

mealtime *shokuji no jikan*

mean: Do you m. it? *Hontō ni?*
  What does this m.? *Kore wa dō yū imi desu ka?*
  What do you m.? *Nan to yū imi desu ka?*

mean: He's m. *Kare wa ijiwaru desu.*

measles *hashika*

measure: tape m. *makijaku*

measuring cup *mejā-kappu*

meat *niku*

meatballs *mīto-bōru*

meat market *nikuya*

mechanic (auto) *shūrikō*

medicine *kusuri*

medicine cabinet *kusuri-todana*

medicine dropper *tenteki-yaku*

mediocre *nami no*

medium (of broiled steak): Make mine m., please. *Midiamu ni yaite kudasai.*

medium rare (of broiled steak): Make mine m. r., please. *Midiamu-reā ni yaite kudasai.*

meeting: It was nice m. you. *O-me ni kakarete ureshū gozaimashita.*

meeting *kaigi*

melon *meron*

melting: It's m. *Tokete imasu.*

memo pad *memo-chō*

menopause *gekkei-heisa*

men's room *o-benjo*
  Where's the m. r.? *O-benjo wa doko desu ka?*

menstruation *gekkei*

mental hospital *seishin-byōin*

mention: Don't m. it. (You're welcome.) *Dō*

itashimashite.

menu *menyū*
　Bring me the m., please.
　Menyū o kudasai.

merchandise *shōhin*

merchant *shōnin*

Merry Christmas! *Kurisumasu o-medetō!*

merry-go-round *kaiten-mo-
kuba*

message *messēji*
　I have (there's) a m. for
　you. *O-katozuke ga ari-
masu.*

messenger *messenjā*

metal *kane*

meter *mētoru*
　a m. of ... *ichimētoru* (see
　also p. 171, Liquid and
　Linear Measures)

mezzanine *chū-nikai*

microphone *maikurohōn*

middle-aged *chūnen no*

middle school *chūgakkō*

midnight *mayonaka*

migraine *henzutsū*

mildew *kabi*

milk *miruku*
　a glass of m. *miruku ippai*
　a liter of m. *miruku
ichirittoru*

butterm. *batā-miruku*

chocolate m. *chokorēto-
miruku*

condensed m. *kondensu-
miruku*

dried skim m. *konamiru-
ku*

evaporated m. *eba-miruku*

skim m. *dasshi-miruku*

million (one) *hyakuman*

milk shake *miruku-sēki*

mind: Did you change your
　m.? *Kangae-naoshima-
shita ka?*
　I've changed my m. *Kan-
gae-naoshimashita.*

mind: Do you m. if I smoke?
　*Tabako o sutte mo ii
desu ka?*
　I don't m. *Kamaimasen.*
　Never m.! *Dōzo go-shim-
pai naku!*

mine: Is it m.? *Watashi no
desu ka?*
　It's m. *Watashi no desu.*
　It's not m. *Watashi no de
wa arimasen.*

mineral oil *minereru oiru*

mineral water *tansansui*

minimum *saishōgen*

mint (herb) *hakka*

minute (a) *ippun*
    a m. ago *ippun mae*
    Just a m.! *Chotto matte kudasai!*
    Wait a m.! *Chotto matte kudasai!*

mirror *kagami*
    magnifying m. *kakudai-kyō*
    rearview m. *bakku-mirā*
    3-way m. *sammenkyō*

miscarriage (medical) *ryūzan*

misdeal *kubari-machigai*

Miss *-san* (after surname)

mist *kasumi*

mistake *machigai*

mistaken: I'm m. *Watashi wa machigatte imasu.*
    Aren't you m.? *Anata wa machigatte imasen ka?*

misty: It's m. out. *Kiri ga kakatte imasu.*

mittens *yubinashi-tebukuro*

mixer (electric) *mikisā*

mixing bowl *bōru*

mix-up *konran*

modern *kindaiteki na*

modest *kenson na*

moist *shimetta*

molar *kyūshi*

molasses *tōmitsu*

mom *mama*

Monday *Getsuyōbi*

money *okane* (see also p. 168, Money Conversion Tables)

money order *kawase*

monkey *saru*

monkey wrench *monki-supanā*

monotonous *tanchō na*

month *tsuki*
    all m. *ikkagetsu-kan*
    a m. ago *ikkagetsu mae*
    every m. *maigetsu*
    last m. *sengetsu*
    next m. *raigetsu*
    once a m. *ikkagetsu ni ichido*
    this m. *kongetsu*
    twice a m. *ikkagetsu ni nido* (see also p. 165 for Months of the Year and Counting Months)

monthly *maigetsu*

monthly payment *tsuki-barai*

monument *kinenhi*

moon *tsuki*
    full m. *mangetsu*
    half-m. *hangetsu*

new m. *shingetsu*
moonlight *gekkō*
mop (for dust) *yukafuki-moppu*
mop (wet) *zōkin* (no handle)
more *motto*
  a little m. *mō sukoshi*
  Have some m., please. *Mō sukoshi ikaga desu ka?*
  Is there any m.? *Mada arimasu ka?*
  many m. *motto takusan*
  May I have some m.? *Mō sukoshi itadaite mo ii desu ka?*
  much m. *motto takusan*
  No m., thank you. *Kekkō desu.*
  once m. *mō ichido*
  one m. *mō hitotsu*
  some m. *motto takusan*
  There isn't any m. *Mō arimasen.*
  Will you have some m.? *Mō sukoshi ikaga desu ka?*
more or less *tashō*
morning *asa*
  all m. *gozen-chū*
  during the m. *gozen-chū*

every m. *maiasa*
Good m.! *O-hayō gozai-masu!*
this m. *kesa*
tomorrow m. *ashita no asa*
yesterday m. *kinō no asa*
mortgage *teitō*
mosquito *ka*
mosquito bite *ka ni sasareta ato*
mosquito net *kaya*
moth *ga*
moth balls *nafutarin*
mother (his, her, your) *o-kāsan*
  (my) *haha*
mother-in-law (his, her, your) *o-shūtome-san*
  (my) *shūtome*
motor *mōtā*
motorbike *mōtā-baiku*
motorboat *mōtā-bōto*
motorcycle *ōtobai*
motorman (street car) *un-tenshi*
motor scooter *sukūtā*
mould (fungus) *kabi*
mouldy *kabi no haeta*
mountain *yama*
mountain range *sammyaku*
mouse *nezumi*

mousetrap *nezumi-tori*
mouth *kuchi*
mouthful *kuchi ippai*
mouthwash *ugai*
move: Don't m.! *Ugokanai yō ni!*
movie *eiga*
movie actor *eiga-haiyū*
movie camera *mūbī-ka-mera*
movie theater *eigakan*
moving van *hikkoshi-umpansha*
mower: lawn m. *shiba-kariki*
Mr. *-san* (after surname)
Mrs. *-san* (after surname)
much *takusan*
　　How m. is it? *Ikura desu ka?*
　　How m. is left? *Dono gurai nokotte imasu ka?*
　　too m. *amari takusan*

much more *motto takusan*
mud *doro*
muddy *dorodarake no*
muffin *maffin*
muffin tin *mafuin-yaki*
muffler (car and scarf) *mafurā*
mumps *otafuku-kaze*
museum *hakubutsukan*
mushroom *ki no ko*
　　dried m. *hoshi-shiitake*
music *ongaku*
musician *ongakuka*
muslin *mosurin*
mustache *hige*
mustard *karashi*
my *watashi no*
myself: Can I do it m.? *Watashi ni dekimasu ka?*
　　I can do it m. *Watashi ni dekimasu.*
　　I can't do it m. *Watashi ni wa dekimasen.*

N

nail (hardware) *kugi*
nail: fingern. *yubi no tsume*

toen. *ashi no tsume*
nail clippers *tsume-kiri*

nail file *tsume-yasuri*
nail polish *manikyua*
nail-polish remover *jokō-eki*
naked *hadaka no*
name *namae*
  first n. *namae*
  Give me your n. and address. *O-namae to go-jūsho o o-negai shimasu.*
  Here's my n. and address. *Kore wa watashi no namae to jūsho desu.*
  last n. *myōji*
  maiden n. *kyūsei*
  My name is .... *Watashi wa ... to mōshimasu.*
  What's your n.? *O-namae wa nan to osshaimasu ka?*
napkin *nafukin*
napkin ring *nafukin-sashi*
narrow *semai*
narrow-minded *kokoro no semai*
national park *kokuritsu-kōen*
native *tochi no hito*
naughty: Don't be n.! *Itazura shite wa ikemasen!*
  That's n.! *Dame desu, yo!*
naughty child *itazurakko*

nausea *hakike*
nauseated: I feel n. *Hakike ga shimasu.*
navel *o-heso*
navel orange *nēburu*
near *chikai*
nearby *chikaku ni*
near-sighted *kingan no*
neat *tansei na*
necessary: Is it n.? *Hitsuyō desu ka?*
  It's n. *Hitsuyō desu.*
  It's not n. *Hitsuyō de wa arimasen.*
neck (of the body) *kubi*
  I have a stiff n. *Kubi o nechigaemashita.*
neck (of a dress) *eri-guri*
necklace *nekkuresu*
necktie *nekutai*
need: Do you n. any? *Irimasu ka?*
  I don't n. any. *Irimasen.*
  I n. some. *Irimasu.*
needle *hari*
negligee *negurije*
negligent *darashinai*
Negro *Kokujin*
neighbor *o-tonari*
neighborhood *kinjo*
neighboring *tonari no*

nephew (his, her, your) *oigosan*
  (my) *oi*
nerve-racking: It's n. *Kibone ga oremasu.*
nervous *shinkeishitsu na*
nervous breakdown *shinkei-suijaku*
neurotic *noirōze*
Never! *Tonde mo nai!*
Never again! *Mō takusan!*
Never mind. *Dōzo goshimpai naku.*
new *atarashii*
newlyweds *shinkon-fūfu*
news *nyūsu*
newspaper *shimbun*
newspaper boy (who delivers) *shimbun-haitatsu*
newsreel *nyūsu-eiga*
New Year: Happy N. Y.! *Shinnen o-medetō gozaimasu!*
New Year's Day *ganjitsu*
New Year's Eve *ōmisoka*
next *tsugi no*
next door *tonari*
next month *raigetsu*
next time *kondo*
next to last *saigo kara nibamme*

next week *raishū*
next year *rainen*
nice *ii*
nickname *adana*
niece (his, her, your) *o-meigosan*
  (my) *mei*
night *yoru*
  all n. *yodōshi*
  during the n. *yonaka*
  every n. *maiban*
  Good n.! *O-yasumi nasai!*
  last n. *sakuban*
  tomorrow n. *ashita no ban*
nightcap (drink) *banshaku*
night club *naito-kurabu*
nightgown *nemaki*
nightmare *akumu*
night table *beddo no wakitēburu*
nine (items) *kokonotsu* (see also p. 163, Numbers and Counting)
nipple (rubber) *o-shaburi*
No! (Don't do that!) *Dame!*
No. (I don't like it.) *Iie.*
No. (That's wrong.) *Chigaimasu.*
No, thank you. (I don't care for any [more].) *Kekkō desu.*

nobody *dare mo*
noise *zatsuon*
noisy *yakamashii*
No kidding! *Jōdan deshō!*
no more *mō takusan*
  There is n. m. *Mō arimasen.*
nonchalant *mutonchaku na*
noncommissioned officer *kashikan*
noodles (J.) *o-udon*
noodles (W.) *shimokawa*
noon *hiru*
  this n. *kyō no hiru*
  tomorrow n. *ashita no hiru*
  yesterday n. *kinō no hiru*
no one *dare mo*
noontime *shōgo*
north *kita*
nose *hana*
nosebleed *hanaji*
  I have a n. *Hanaji ga demasu.*
nose drops *hanagusuri*
nostril *hana no ana*
notebook *nōto*
nothing *nani mo*
no trump (bridge) *kirifuda nashi*
not yet *mada*

novel (book) *shōsetsu*
novelist *shōsetsuka*
November *Jūichi-gatsu*
novocaine *nobokēn*
now *ima*
nowadays *kono goro*
now & then *toki-doki*
nowhere *doko ni mo*
nude *hadaka no*
numb *shibireta*
number *bangō*
  cabin n. *senshitsu-bangō*
  flight n. *hikō-bangō*
  room n. *heya-bangō*
  seat n. *zaseki-bangō*
  telephone n. *denwa-bangō*
  track (RR) n. ... *bansen* (see also p. 163, Numbers and Counting)
nurse *kangofu-san* (see also p.155, Health Problems)
nursemaid *uba*
nursery *kodomo-beya*
  day n. *takujisho*
  tree n. *naegi-shitateba*
nursery school *hoikuen*
nursing bottle *honyūbin*
nut (hardware) *natto*
nut *kinomi*
  almond *āmondo*
  chestn. *kuri*

pean. *pinattsu*
pecan *pīkan*
waln. *kurumi*
nutcracker *kurumi-wari*

nutmeg *nattomeggu*
nylon *nairon*
nylons (stockings) *sutokkin-gu*

O

obedient *jūjun na*
oblong *chōhōkei*
obstetrician *sanfujin-ka*
occupied: Is this seat o.? *Kono seki wa aite imasu ka?*
    This seat is o. *Kimasu.*
ocean *umi*
October *Jū-gatsu*
octopus *tako*
oculist *me-isha*
odd (strange) That's o. *Okashii.*
odd number *kisū*
odor *kaori*
Of course! (I will!) *Kashikomarimashita!*
Of course! (That's right!) *Mochiron!*
off & on *toki-doki*
office *jimusho*

    branch o. *shiten*
    head o. *honten*
office building *biru*
officer (military) *shōkō*
often *tabi-tabi*
oil *abura*
    fuel o. *keiyu*
    lubricating o. *junkatsuyu*
    mineral o. *minereru oiru*
    olive o. *oribu-oiru*
    salad o. *sarada-oiru*
    tempura o. (for cooking) *tempura-abura*
oil filter (car) *oiru-fuirutā*
oil painting *abura-e*
ointment *nuri-gusuri*
O.K. *ōkē*
old (of persons) *toshiyori*
    How o. are you? *O-ikutsu desu ka?*
old (of things) *furui*

How o. is it? *Dono gurai furui desu ka?*

Old Fashioned (drink) *ōru-do-fuasshon*

old-fashioned *ryūkō-okure no*

old maid (unmarried woman) *ōrudo-misu*

olive *orību*

olive oil *orību-oiru*

omelet *omuretsu*

on ... *no ue ni*

once *ichido*

all at o. *ippen ni*

once a day *ichinichi ni ichido*

once a month *ikkagetsu ni ichido*

once a week *isshūkan ni ichido*

once a year *ichinen ni ichido*

once more *mō ichido*

Once upon a time *Mukashi, mukashi*

one (item) *hitotsu* (see also p. 163, Numbers and Counting)

one by one *hitotsu-zutsu*

one more *mō hitotsu*

one quarter *yombun-no-ichi*

one-way street *ippō-tsūkō*

one-way ticket *katamichi-kippu*

one-way traffic *ippō-tsūkō*

onion (round) *tamanegi*, (long) *naganegi*

only: Is that the o. one? *Sore hitotsu dake desu ka?*

That's the o. one. *Sore hitotsu dake desu.*

on order *chūmon-chū*

on time *jikan-dōri ni*

on top of ... *no ue ni*

open: Is it o.? *Aite imasu ka?*

It's o. *Aite imasu.*

It's not o. *Aite imasen.*

What time does it o.? *Nanji ni akemasu ka?*

opener: bottle o. *sen-nuki*

can o. *kan-kiri*

open house (reception) *ō-pun-hausu*

opening (job) *shūshokuguchi*

Open the window (door), please. *Mado (doa) o akete kudasai.*

operation (surgical) *shujutsu*

operator (telephone) *kōkan-*

shu

opponent *aite*

opposite (the) *hantai*

opposite direction *hantai no hō*

opposite side *hantai-gawa*

or *muta wa*

orange (color) *orenji-iro*

orange (fruit) *orenji*

　navel o. *nēburu*

　tangerine *mikan*

orangeade *orenji-ēdo*

orange juice *orenji-jūsu*

orangewood stick *amakawa-hagi*

orchestra *ōkesutora*

orchestra seat *tokutō-seki*

order: made-to-o. *chūmon-atsurae*

　on o. *chūmon-chū*

　out of o. *koshō-chū*

Orient *Tōyō*

Oriental *Tōyō no*, (person) *Tōyōjin*

original *orijinaru*

orphan *minashigo*

orphan asylum *koji-in*

other *hoka no*

other (the) *betsu no*

Ouch! *A itai!*

our *watashitachi no*

ours: Is it o.? *Watashitachi no desu ka?*

　It's not o. *Watashitachi no de wa arimasen.*

　It's o. *Watashitachi no desu.*

out: Get o.! *Dete ikinasai!*

　in & o. *detari haittari*

outboard motor *mōtābōto-yō enjin*

outdoors *yagai*

outlet (electrical) *konsento*

out of breath: Are you o. o. b.? *Iki ga kiremashita ka?*

　I'm o. o. b. *Iki ga kiresō ni narimashita.*

out of order *koshō-chū*

outside ... *no sotogawa ni*

outside (outdoors) *yagai*

oval *tamago-gata no*

oven *ōbun*

oven mitt *ōbun-tebukuro*

oven proof (cookware) *tempi-yō*

oven timer *ōbun-taimā*

over ... *no ue ni*

overboard *sengai ni*

　Man o.! *Dare ka tobikonda (ochita) zo!*

overcoat *ōbā*

overcooked *yaki-sugita*
overcrowded *man·in*
overdose *karyō*
overexposed (film) *roshutsu-kajō*
overhead (running expenses) *keijō-hi*
overhead (above) ... *no ue ni*
over here *kochira*
overnight *ippaku*
overpass *gādo*
overseas *kaigai*
overseas call (telephone) *kokusai-denwa*
overshoes *ōbā-shūzu*
over there *achira*
overtime *zangyō*
overtrick (bridge) *ōbātorikku*
overweight (baggage) *jūryō-chōka*
overweight (person) *futori-sugi*
overwork *hataraki-sugi*
oxfords (shoes) *tangutsu*
oyster *kaki*

P

Pacific Ocean *Taiheiyō*
pacifier (for babies) *o-shaburi*
pack (of cards) *hitokumi*
pack of cigarettes (chewing gum) *tabako (chūingamu) hitohako*
package *kozutsumi*
pad (for writing) *memo*
padded bra *patto-iri burajā*
paddy field *tambo*
padlock *jōmae*
page (of a book) *pēji*
pail *baketsu*
pain *itami*
  I have a p. here. *Koko ga itai desu.*
painful: Is it p.? *Itai desu ka?*
  It's not p. *Itaku nai desu.*
  It's p. *Itai desu.*
paint *penki*
paintbrush *penki-burashi*
painter (artist) *gaka*
painting *kaiga; e*
paint roller *penki-rōrā*

paint thinner *shinnā*

pair of gloves *tebukuro hitokumi*

pair of shoes *kutsu issoku*

pair of stockings *kutsushita issoku*

pair of trousers *zubon ippon*

pair of undershorts *pantsu ichimai*

pajamas *pajama*

Pakistan *Pakisutan*

pal *nakama*

pale *aojiroi*

   You look p. *Aoi kao o shite imasu.*

palm (of the hand) *tenohira*

Palm Sunday *Shuro no Nichiyōbi*

pan *furaipan*

   dishp. *arai-oke*

pancake *hotto-kēki*

pansy *sanshiki-sumire*

panties *panti*

pantry *chozō-shitsu*

pants *zubon*

   a pair of p. *zubon ippon*

   underp. *zubonshita*

panty girdle *pantī-gādoru*

paper *kami*

   a sheet of p. *kami ichimai*

   carbon p. *kābon-shi*

   Japanese p. (handmade) *wa-shi*

   newsp. *shimbun*

   sandp. *kami-yasuri*

   tissue p. *chirigami*

   toilet p. *toiretto-pēpā*

   tracing p. *seizu-yōshi*

   typing p. *taipu-yōshi*

   wallp. *kabe-gami*

   wax p. *rō-gami*

   wrapping p. *tsutsumi-gami*

   writing p. *binsen*

paperback (book) *bunko-bon*

paper bag *kami-bukuro*

paper clip *kurippu*

paper doll *kami-ningyō*

paperhanger *kyōjiya*

paperweight *bunchin*

paprika *papurika*

parade *parēdo*

paraffin *parafin*

parakeet *inko*

parallel *heikō na*

parasol (J.) *higasa*

parcel *kozutsumi*

pardon: I beg your p. *Gomen nasai.*

Pardon me. *Sumimasen.*

parents (his, her, your) *go-ryōshin*

   (my) *ryōshin*

paring knife *kawamuki-hō-chō*

park *kōen*

    national p. *kokuritsu-kōen*

parking lot *chūshajō*

parsley *paseri*

part (hair) *wakeme*

partner *pātonā*

part-time *pāto-taimu*

    p.-t. employment *arubaito*

party (fête) *pātī*

    birthday p. *tanjō-pātī*

    bridge p. *burijji-pātī*

    dinner p. *dinnā-pātī*

party bridge *pātī-burijji*

pass (identification card) *mibun-shōmeisho*

passenger (on train, street-car) *jōkyaku*

passenger (on ship) *senkya-ku*

passenger train *kyakusha*

passport *pasupōto*

past (the) *kako*

    in the p. *kako ni oite*

paste *nori*

    toothp. *hamigaki*

pastime *goraku*

pastry (J.) *o-kashi*, (W.) *yō-kashi*

pastry shop *o-kashiya*

patent leather *enameru-gawa*

path *roji*

patient (medical) *kanja*

patient *shimbō-zuyoi*

    Be p.! *Gaman shinasai!*

pattern (for dresses, etc.) *kata ; katagami*

payday *kyūryōbi*

peace *heiwa*

peaceful *heiwa na*

peach *momo*

peanut *pīnattsu*

peanut butter *pīnattsu-batā*

peanut-butter sandwich *pīnattsu-batā sandoitchi*

pear (J.) *nashi*, (W.) *seiyō-nashi*

pearl *shinju*

peas *mame*

pea soup *mame-sūpu*

pecan *pīkan*

pediatrician *shōnika-i*

pen (for writing) *pen*

    ball-point p. *bōru-pen*

pencil *empitsu*

pencil sharpener *empitsu-kezuri*

penicillin *penishirin*

penthouse *pento-hausu*

people *hitobito* (see p. 164 for

counting people)
pepper (ground black) *koshō*, (green) *pīman*
peppermint *pepāminto*
pepper shaker *koshō-ire*
percent *pāsento*
perfume *kōsui*
perhaps *tabun*
permanent wave *pāma*
persimmon *kaki*
dried p. *hoshi-gaki*
person *hito*
perspiration *ase*
perspiring: I'm p. *Ase o kaite imasu.*
petunia *pechunia*
pew *kyōkai no seki*
pharmacy *kusuriya*
Philippine Islands *Fuirippin*
phone *denwa*
phone call *denwa*
phone number *denwa-bangō*
phonograph *chikuonki*
phonograph record *rekōdo*
photograph *shashin*
photo studio *shashinya*
photo supply shop *kamera-ya*
piano *piano*

pickles (J.) *o-tsukemono*
picnic *pikunikku*
picture *e*
picture (photograph) *shashin*
picture frame *gakubuchi*
picture postcard *ehagaki*
pie *pai*
apple p. *appuru-pai*
chocolate p. *chokorēto-pai*
custard p. *purin-pai*
lemon p. *remon-pai*
piece: a p. of bread (cake) *pan (kēki) hitokire*
a p. of paper *kami ichimai*
piecrust *pai no kawa*
pie tin *pai-zara*
pig *buta*
pigskin (leather) *butagawa*
pigtail (braid) *o-sage*
pill *gan・yaku*
pillow *makura*
pillowcase *makura-kabā*
pilot *pairotto*
pilot light (gas stove) *tenka-sen*
pimple *nikibi*
pin (bowling) *pin*
pin: safety p. *anzen-pin*
straight p. *machi-bari*
pinball (J.) *pachinko*

pineapple *painappuru*

pineapple juice *pain-jūsu*

ping-pong *pimpon*

pink *pinku*

pinking shears *pinkingu-basami*

pipe (for smoking) *paipu*

pipe (metal) *tekkan*

pipe cleaner *paipu-kurīnā*

pipe rack *paipu-tate*

piston *p:suton*

pit (kernel) *tane*

pitcher (for liquids) *mizu-sashi*

    cream p. *kurimu-ire*

pity: I p. you. *O-kinodoku ni omoimasu.*

    What a p. ! *Oshii koto desu !*

place mat (for table) *tēburu-matto*

plaid (material) *kōshijima*

plain *muji no*

plank *ita*

plaster cast *gibusu*

plate (dish) *o-sara*

platform: RR station p. *hōmu*

platform ticket *nyūjōken*

platter (dish) *ōzara*

play (theatrical) *shibai*

playboy *purēbōi*

playground *undōjō*

playing card *torampu*

playmate *asobi-tomodachi*

playpen *purēpen*

Please. (Take it or Go ahead.) *Dōzo.*

    (Bring me or Give me.) *Kudasai.*

    (Help me or Wait on me.) *O-negai shimasu.*

pleat *hida*

pliers *penchi*

plug (electric) *sashikomi*

plum *puramu*

plumber (Water Dept.) *sui-dōkyoku*

plump *futotta*

plum tree (flowering) *ume no ki*

plywood *beniya-ita*

p.m. *gogo*

pneumonia *hai-en*

poached egg *otoshi-tamago*

P.O. box *shisho-bako*

pocket *poketto*

pocketbook *handobaggu*

poem *shi*

poet *shijin*

poetry *shīka*

pointed *togatta*

points (car motor) *pointo*

poised: She's very p. *Jōhin na kata desu.*

poison *doku*

poison sumac (Japanese lacquer) *urushi*

police *keisatsu*

police box *kōban*

policeman *o-mawari-san*
  Call a p., please. *O-mawari-san o yonde kudasai.*

police station *keisatsusho*

policy: insurance p. *hoken-shōken*

polish: brass p. *shinchū-migaki*
  furniture p. *kagu no tsuya-dashi*
  nail p. *manikyua*
  silver p. *gin-migaki*
  shoe p. *kutsuzumi*

polish remover (nail polish) *jokō-eki*

polite *teinei na*

pond *ike*

pony *ko-uma*

ponytail (hairdo) *ponītēru*

pool (for swimming) *pūru*

poor *mazushii*

poor sport *kujike-yasui*

popcorn *poppukōn*

Pope *Rōmahō-ō*

popsicle *aisu-kyandē*

popular: He (she) is very p. *Ano hito wa ninki ga arimasu.*
  You're very p. *Ninki ga arimasu, ne.*

porcelain *jiki*

pork *butaniku*

pork chop *pōku-choppu*

pork cutlet *pōku-katsuretsu*

pork roast *yaki-buta*

porter *akabō*

post (mil.) *kichi*
  off p. *kichi no soto de*
  on p. *kichi no naka de*

postage stamp *kitte*

postbox *yūbimbako*

postcard *hagaki*

postman *yūbin-haitatsu*

post office *yūbinkyoku*

pot (for cooking) *o-nabe*
  teap. (J.) *kyūsu*, (W.) *tī-potto*

potato *jagaimo*
  baked p. *yaki-jagaimo*
  baked sweet p. *yaki-imo*
  boiled p. *yudeta-jagaimo*
  sweet p. *satsuma-imo*

potato chips *poteto-chippu*

potatoes: fried p. *poteto-furai*

mashed p. *masshu-poteto*
potato salad *poteto-sarada*
pot holder *ōbun-tebukuro*
pottery *setomono*
poultry (meat) *tori-niku*
poverty *hinkon; bimbō*
powder: face p. *o-shiroi*
  soap p. *kona-sekken*
  tooth p. *ha-migakiko*
powder base (cosmetic)
  keshō-shita
powdered sugar *kona-zatō*
powder puff *pafu*
practical joke *waru-fuzake*
prayer *inori*
prayer beads (Buddhist)
  juzu
prefectural office: Hokkai-
  dō *dō-chō*
  Kyōto & Ōsaka *fu-chō*
  Tōkyō *to-chō*
  all others *ken-chō*
preferred stock *yūsenkabu*
pregnant *ninshin shita*
prep school *yobi-kō*
prescription *shohō*
present (gift) *okurimono*
present (time) *genzai*
president (of a company)
  shachō
pretty *kirei na*

pretzel *purettseru*
price *nedan*
price of admission *nyūjōryō*
prickly heat *kabure*
priest (Buddhist) *o-bō-san*
  (Shintō) *kannushi-san*
  (Christian) *shimpu-san*
print (woodblock) *hanga*
print: out of p. *zeppan no*
printed fabric *sarasa*
printing *insatsu*
prison *keimusho*
private *shiteki na*
private room *hitori-kiri no
  heya*
private school *shiritsu-gakkō*
profession *shokugyō*
professor *kyōju*
profile *yokogao*
program *puroguramu*
projector (movie) *eishaki*,
  (slide) *gentōki*
promise (a) *yakusoku*
Promise! *Yakusoku desu,
  ne!*
promissory note *yakusoku-
  tegata*
prompt *subayai*
prostitute *baishunfu*

protein *tampakushitsu*
Protestant *Shinkyōto*
proud *gōman na*
prune (cooked with syrup)
　nikomi-puramu
　(dried) *hoshi-puramu*
prune juice *puramu-jūsu*
pruning shears *sentei-basa-
　mi*
psalm *shihen*
psychiatrist *seishinka-i*
ptomaine poisoning *puto-
　mēn-chūdoku*
public *kōshū no*
　in p. *ōyake ni*
public toilet *kyōdō-benjo*
pudding *purin*
puddle *mizu-tamari*
Pull! *Hippatte kudasai!*
pullover sweater *sētā*
pump (shoe) *pampusu*
pump (for tires) *kūki-ire*
pun *share*
punch (beverage) *ponchi*
punctual *kichōmen*
punishment *batsu*

puppet *ayatsuri-ningyō*
puppy *ko-inu*
purchase (a) *kaimono*
pure *junsui na*
purebred *junketsu no*
pure silk *kinu*
purple *murasaki no*
purpose: on p. *waza to*
purse (handbag) *hando-bag-
　gu*
　change p. *kozeni-ire*
　evening p. *yakaiyō hando-
　baggu*
purser's office (on ship-
　board) *pāsā no ofisu*
pus *umi*
Push! *Oshite kudasai!*
Put it away! *Shimatte oite
　kudasai!*
Put it back! *Modoshite oite
　kudasai!*
Put it down! *Oroshite kuda-
　sai!*
puzzle: crossword p. *kuro-
　suwādo-pazuru*
　jigsaw p. *hame-e*

Q

quarrel *kenka*
quarter: one q. *yombun-no-ichi*
  three q. *yombun-no-san*
quarter of an hour *jūgo-funkan*
queen (playing card) *kuīn*
queer (strange) *hen na*
question (a) *shitsumon*
  Do you have a q.? *Nani ka go-shitsumon ga arimasu*
  ka?
  May I ask you a q.? *Shitsumon shite ii desu ka?*
quick *hayai*
  Be q.! *Hayaku!*
quickly: Come q.! *Hayaku kite kudasai!*
quick-tempered *okorippoi*
quiet *shizuka na*
  Be q.! *Shizuka ni shinasai!*

R

racetrack (horse) *keibajō*
rack: pipe r. *paipu-tate*
  towel r. *taoru-kake*
racket: tennis r. *raketto*
radiator *dambō-sōchi*
  car r. *rajiētā*
radio (receiver) *rajio*
  transistor r. *toranjisutā-rajio*
radio announcer *anaunsā*
radio station *hōsōkyoku*
radish *hatsuka-daikon*
rag (for cleaning) *fukin*
railroad *tetsudō*

railroad car *kyakusha*

railroad crossing *fumi-kiri*

railroad station *eki*

railroad track *senro*

railroad train *kisha*

rain *ame*

Do you think it's going to r.? *Ame ga furu to omoimasu ka?*

I don't think it's going to r. *Ame ga furu to wa omoimasen.*

I think it's going to r. *Ame ga furu deshō.*

raincoat *rēnkōto*

raining: Is it r.? *Ame ga futte imasu ka?*

It's stopped r. *Ame ga yamimashita.*

It's not r. *Ame wa futte imasen.*

It's r. *Ame ga futte imasu.*

It's r. cats and dogs. *Ame ga zāzā futte imasu.*

rainstorm *arashi*

rain water *ama-mizu*

rainy season *tsuyu*

raisin *hoshi-budō*

raisin bread *budō-pan*

rake (garden, bamboo) *kumade*

(metal) *rēki*

rape *bōkō*

rare (of broiled steak) *nama-yake no*

Make mine r., please. *Nama-yake ni shite kudasai.*

rash (eruption) *jimmashin*

raspberry *ki-ichigo*

rat *nezumi*

rattan *tō*

rattle (child's) *garagara*

rattrap *nezumi-tori*

raw (uncooked) *nama no*

raw egg *nama-tamago*

raw silk *ki-ito*

rayon *rēyon*

razor *kami-sori*

razor blade *kami-sori no ha*

ready: Are you r.? *Jumbi wa ii desu ka?*

I'm not r. *Mada desu.*

I'm r. *Jumbi ga dekimashita.*

It's all r. *Jumbi ga dekimashita.*

When will it be r.? *Itsu dekimasu ka?*

When will you be r.? *Itsu jumbi ga dekimasu ka?*

ready-made (clothes) *kisei-*

fuku

ready-mix *mikkusu*

ready-to-wear (clothes) *bu-ra-sagari*

real *hontō no*

real estate *fudōsan*

real-estate agent *fudōsan·ya*

rearview mirror *bakku-mirā*

receipt *uke-tori*

recently *chika-goro*

recipe *chōri-hō*

record (phonograph) *rekōdo*
   forty-five r.p.m. *yonjūgo-kaiten*
   long-playing r. *erupī-rekō-do*

recording tape *rokuon-tēpu*

record player *rekōdo-purē-yā*

recreation *rekurēshon*

recreation area *yūenchi*

red *akai*

Red Cross *Sekijūji*

redhead *akage*

red light (traffic) *aka-shingō*

red pepper *tōgarashi*

red tape *o-yakusho-fū*

reduced (as sale goods) *waribiki no*

red wine *reddo-wain*

refined (well-mannered) *jō-hin na*

refreshments *seiryō-inryō*

refrigerator *reizōko*

register: (at the ward office) Where do I r.? *Doko de tōroku shimasu ka?*

registered letter *kakitome*

registration: alien r. *gaiko-kujin tōroku*
   car r. *jidōsha-tōroku*

regular *ittei no*

rehearsal *rihāsaru*

relaxed *kutsuroida*

remember: Do you r.? *O-boete imasu ka?*
   I don't r. *Oboete imasen.*
   I r. *Oboete imasu.*

remover (solvent) *hakurizai*

renew: I want to r. my visa. *Biza o kōshin shitai desu.*

renewal (subscription) *sai-keiyaku*

rent (house, apt.) *yachin*, (room) *heyadai*

rental agent *fudōsan·ya*

rental agent fee *tesūryō*

Repeat that, please. *Mō ichido itte kudasai.*

report card (from school)

    seisekihyō

reservation *yoyaku*

reserved (shy) *otonashii*

reserved seat *shitei-seki*

reserved table *yoyaku-seki*

resort *hoyō*
    ski r. *sukī-jō*
    summer r. *hishochi*

rest (a) *yasumi*

rest (the) *nokori*

restaurant (J.) *ryōriya*, (W.) *resutoran*

return address *henshin-jūsho*

return trip *ōfuku-ryokō*

reverse (the) *hantai*
    in r. (car) *bakku*

revolving door *kaiten-doa*

revue (dance act) *rebyū*

reward *hōbi*

rheumatism *ryūmachi*

rhubarb *rūbābu*

rib *rokkotsu*

ribbon *ribon*
    typewriter r. *taipuraitā-ribon*

rice (cooked) *gohan*
    a bowl of r. *gohan ichizen*

rice (uncooked) *kome*
    a kilo of r. *kome ichikiro*

rice paddy *tambo*

rich *kanemochi no*

riding boots *jōba-gutsu*

riding breeches *jōba-zubon*

riding habit *jōba-fuku*

riding school *jōba-gakkō*

right: All r.! *Yoroshii!*
    I'm r. *Machigatte inai tsumori desu.*
    Is it all r.? *Yoroshii desu ka?*
    It's (that's) all r. *Daijōbu desu, yo.*
    That's r. *Sō desu.*
    You're r. *Sō desu.*

right (opposite of left) *migi*
    on the r. (side) *migi no hō*
    Turn r. *Migi e magatte kudasai.*

right away *sugu ni*
    I'm coming r. a. *Sugu ikimasu.*

right-handed *migi-kiki*

right side *migi no hō*

rind *kawa*

ring (for the finger) *yubiwa*
    engagement r. *kon·yaku-yubiwa*
    wedding r. *kekkon-yubiwa*

rinse (color, for hair) *karā-rinsu*

rinsing (a) *rinsu*

ripe (as of fruit) *jukushita*
risqué joke *waidan*
river *kawa*
river bank *dote*
road *dōro*
road map *dōro-chizu*
roast (meat) *rōsuto*
roast beef *rōsuto-bīfu*
roast chicken *rōsuto-chikin*
roast duck *rōsuto-dakku*
roast turkey *rōsuto-tākī*
rock & roll *rokkunrōru*
rock garden *sekitei*
rocking chair *rokkingu-cheā*
rod: curtain r. *kāten-bō*
　　curtain r. (grooved for drapes) *kāten-rēru*
roll (bread) *rōru-pan*
roller (for hair) *rōrā*
roller (for painting) *rōrā*
roller skates *rōrā-sukēto*
rolling pin *membō*
romantic *romanchikku*
roof *yane*
rooftop *okujō*
room (space) *basho*
room (in a house) *heya*
room & board *geshuku*
room number *heya-bangō*
root (of a plant) *ne*
rope *rōpu*

rosary beads *rozario*
rose *bara*
rosebush *bara no ki*
rouge *beni*
rough (surface, texture) *arai*
rough (person) *arappoi*
round *marui*
round-shouldered *nadegata no*
round-trip ticket *ōfuku-kippu*
rubber (bridge) *shōbu*
rubber band *gomu*
rubber boots *gomugutsu*
rubbing alcohol *arukōru*
rubbish *garakuta*
rudder *kaji*
rude (impolite) *shitsurei na*
rug *jūtan*
ruler (for measuring) *monosashi*
rum *ramu*
rumor *uwasa*
run (in nylons) *densen*
run: Don't r.! *Hashitte wa ikemasen!*
rush hour *rasshu-awā*
rust *sabi*
rusty *sabita*
rye bread *raimugi-pan*

S

saccharin *sakkarin*
sad *kanashii*
saddle *kura*
safe *anzen na*
safety deposit box *kyūkyū-bako*
safety pin *anzen-pin*
safety zone *anzen-chitai*
sail *ho*
sailboat *yotto*
sailor (mil.) *suihei*, (seaman) *funanori*
salad *sarada*
   chicken s. *chikin-sarada*
   fruit s. *furūtsu-sarada*
   potato s. *poteto-sarada*
   tossed green s. *gurin-sarada*
salad bowl *sarada-bōru*
salad dressing *sarada-doresshingu*
salad oil *sarada-oiru*
salary (monthly) *gekkyū*
sale: Is this for s.? *Kore wa uri-mono desu ka?*
   on s. (at a reduced price) *ō-uri-dashi*
salesclerk *ten·in*
saliva *tsuba*
salmon *sake*; *shake*
salt *o-shio*
salt shaker *shio-ire*
salt water *shio-mizu*
salty *karai*
same *onaji*
same thing: Is it the s. t.? *Onaji mono desu ka?*
   It's the s. t. *Onaji mono desu.*
   It's not the s. t. *Onaji mono de wa arimasen.*
sample *mihon*
sanatorium *sanatoryūmu*
sand *suna*
sandal *sandaru*
sandbox *sunaba*
sandpaper *kami-yasuri*
sandwich *sandoitchi*

cheese s. *chīzu-sandoitchi*

chicken s. *chikin-sandoitchi*

egg-salad s. *tamago-sarada sandoitchi*

grilled-cheese s. *chīzu tōsuto*

ham s. *hamu-sandoitchi*

jelly s. *zerī-sandoitchi*

peanut-butter s. *pīnattsubatā sandoitchi*

tuna-fish-salad s. *maguro-sarada sandoitchi*

sandy *sunappoi*

sane *shōki no*

Santa Claus *Santa-kurōsu*

sardine *iwashi*

sash (J.) *obi*

satin *shusu*

satisfied: Are you s.? *Ii desu ka?*

I'm not s. *Mada.*

I'm s. *Ii desu.*

Saturday *Doyōbi*

sauce *sōsu*

saucepan *o-nabe*

saucer (for cup) *uke-zara*

sauerkraut *sawākurauto*

sausage *sōsēji*

savings *chokin; chochiku*

savings account *futsū yokin*

saw (tool) *nokogiri*

Say! *Ano ne!*

say: How do you s. that in Japanese? *Sore wa Nihongo de nan to iimasu ka?*

What did he (she) s.? *Nan to iimashita ka?*

What did you s.? *Nan to osshaimashita ka?*

scallops *hotategai*

scandal *sukyandaru*

scar *kizu-ato*

scarce *sukunai*

scared: Are you s.? *Kowai desu ka?*

I'm not s. *Watashi wa kowaku arimasen.*

I'm s. *Watashi wa kowai desu.*

scarf *eri-maki*

scarf (square, for wrapping) *furoshiki*

scenery (landscape) *keshiki*

schedule *sukejūru*

train s. *ressha-daiya*

school *gakkō*

elementary s. *shōgakkō*

high s. *kōkō*

kindergarten *yōchien*

middle s. (junior high)

   chūgakkō
nursery s. *hoikuen*
prep s. *yobi-kō*
private s. *shiritsu-gakkō*
Sunday s. *Nichiyō-gakkō*
school term *gakki*
scissors *hasami*
   manicure s. *manikyua-ba-
samī*
   nail s. *tsume-kiri-basami*
Scotch (whisky) *Sukotchi*
Scotch & soda *Sukotchi-sōda*
Scotch & water *Sukotchi-
uōtā*
scotch tape *sero-tēpu*
scouring powder *migakiko*
scrambled egg *kaki-tamago*
scrapbook *sukurappu-bukku*
scrap paper *zara-gami*
scratch (a) *kizu*
screen (to keep out flies)
amido
screen (J., folding) *byōbu*
screen (J. translucent door)
shōji
screen (for slide projection)
sukurīn
screw (hardware) *neji*
screwdriver *neji-mawashi*
scroll (J., hanging) *kake-
mono*

sculptor *chōkokuka*
sculpture *chōkoku*
sea *umi*
seafood *kaisambutsu*
seal (stamp) *han*
seam *nui-me*
sea shell *kaigara*
seashore *kaigan*
seasick *funayoi*
   Do you feel s.? *Funayoi
desu ka?*
   I don't feel s. *Funayoi de
wa arimasen.*
   I feel s. *Funayoi ni narimashita.*
season ticket *teiki*
seat (theater, train, etc.)
seki
seat belt *shīto-beruto*
seat number *zaseki-bangō*
seaweed (edible) *nori*
second (the) *dai-ni*
second (time unit) *byō*
second floor *ni-kai*
secondhand *chūburu no*
second hand (on the clock)
byōshin
second helping *o-kawari*
secret *himitsu*
secretary (private) *hisho*
securities (stocks and

bonds) *yūka-shōken*

sedative *chinseizai*

see: I'll s. you later. *Mata ato de.*

I'll s. you tomorrow. *Mata ashita.*

I s. (I understand.) *Waka-rimashita.*

May I s. that? *Sore o misete itadakemasu ka?*

seesaw *shisō*

self-centered *jiko chūshin-teki na*

selfish *rikoteki na*

Don't be s. *Yokubaranai de kudasai.*

senile *rōnen no*

sensible *kemmei na*

separate *betsubetsu no*

Separate checks, please. *Betsubetsu ni kanjō o shite kudasai.*

September *Ku-gatsu*

servant (maid) *mēdo*

servant (man) *bōisan*

service station *gasorin-su-tando (see also* p. 151, At the Service Station)

set (hair) *setto*

set of golf clubs *gorufu-kurabu hitokumi*

set of silver *naifu hōku hitokumi*

seven (items) *nanatsu (see also* p. 163, Numbers and Counting)

several *ikutsu ka no*

sew: Will you s. this, please? *Kore o nutte kudasaimasen ka?*

sewing machine *mishin*

Sew on this button, please. *Kono botan o nuitsukete kudasai.*

sex *sei*

female s. *josei*

male s. *dansei*

shade (from the sun) *hikage*

shade *kage*

lamps. *sutando no kasa*

shadow *kage*

shady *hikage no*

shallow *asai*

shame: That's (it's) a shame. *Sore wa o-kino-doku-sama.*

shampoo (for hair) *shampū*

shampoo-set *shampū-setto*

sharp *surudoi*

Sharpen this knife, please. *Kono naifu o toide kuda-sai.*

shave (a) *hige-sori*

shaver (electric) *denki-kami-sori*

shaving brush *hige-sori burashi*

shaving cream *shēbingu-kurimu*

she *kanojo wa (ga)*

shears: pinking s. *pinkingu-basami*

    pruning s. *sentei-basami*

sheer (material) *sukitōtta*

sheet: bed s. *shītsu*

sheet of paper *kami ichi-mai*

shelf *tana*

shell: egg s. *tamago no kara*

    sea s. *kaigara*

sherbet *shābetto*

Shintoism *Shintō*

ship *fune*

shipwreck *nampa*

shirt *shatsu*

    dress shirt *waishatsu*

    sport s. *supōtsu-shatsu*

    sweat s. *jampā*

    unders. *shitagi*

shiver: It makes me s. *Dokidoki shimasu.*

shivering: I'm s. (with cold). *Samuke ga shima-su.*

shoe *kutsu*

shoebrush *kutsu-burashi*

shoehorn *kutsubera*

shoelace *kutsuhimo*

shoemaker *kutsuya*

shoe polish *kutsuzumi*

shoe repair shop *kutsu-naoshi*

shoes: loafers *mokashin*

    oxfords *tangutsu*

    a pair of s. *kutsu issoku*

    pumps *pampusu*

    sandals *sandaru*

    sneakers *undō-gutsu*

    tennis s. *undō-gutsu*

shoeshine *kutsu-migaki*

shoeshop *kutsuya*

shoetree *kutsugata*

shop (a) *mise*

shopping *kaimono* (see also p. 148, General Shopping Phrases)

shopworn *tanazarashi no*

short (length) *mijikai*

    How s. is it? *Dono gurai mijikai desu ka?*

    It's too s. *Sore wa mijika-sugimasu.*

short (opposite of tall) *hikui*

short circuit *shōto*

shortcut *chikamichi*

shortening (for cooking) *shōtoningu*

Shorten this, please. *Kore o mijikaku shite kudasai.*

shorthand *sokki*

shorts *hanzubon*
unders. *pantsu*

short story *tampen-shōsetsu*

short-tempered *tanki na*

short-waisted *dō ga mijikai*

shot (injection) *chūsha*

shoulder *kata*

shoulder strap (of a slip) *surippu no katahimo*

shovel *shaberu*

show (exhibition) *tenrankai*

show (film) *eiga*

show: I'll s. you how to go. (to taxi driver) *Annai shimasu.*
Let me s. you. *Misete agemashō.*

shower (rain) *niwaka-ame*

shower (bath) *shawā*

shower curtain *shawāyō-kāten*

Show me that, please. *Sore o misete kudasai.*

shrimp *ebi*

shrine (Shintō) *jinja*

shrink: Will this material s.? *Kono kiji wa chiji-mimasu ka?*

shuffle: It's your s. *Anata no kiru ban desu.*

shutter (window) *amado*

shutter (of camera) *shattā*

shy *hazukashii*

Siberia *Shiberiya*

sick: Are you s.? *Byōki desu ka?*
Do you feel s.? *Kibun ga warui desu ka?*
I'm not s. *Byōki de wa arimasen.*
I'm s. *Byōki desu.*
I feel s. *Kibun ga warui desu. (see also p. 155, Health Problems)*

sickness *byōki*

side: on the s. *yoko ni*
the left s. *hidarigawa*
the right s. *migigawa*
the right s. (of material) *omote*
the wrong s. (of material) *ura*

sideboard (buffet) *shokki-todana*

sidewalk *hodō*

sideways *naname ni*

sieve *ura-goshi*
sifter (cooking utensil) *furui*
sigh (a) *tame-iki*
sightseeing *kankō*
sightseeing bus *kankō-basu*
silence *shizukesa*
silk *kinu*
  raw s. (thread) *ki-ito*
silk thread *kinu-ito*
silkworm *kaiko*
sill: doors. *shiki-i*
  windows. *mado-jiki-i*
silly *baka*
silver (metal) *gin*
  a set of s. (flatware) *naifu hōku hitokumi*
silver (money) *ginka*
silver plate *gin-mekki*
silver polish *gin-migaki*
silverware *ginseihin*
simple *kantan na*
sincere *majime na*
singer *kashu*
single (man) *dokushin*
  (woman) *mikon no*
  Are you s.? *O-hitori desu ka?*
  He's s. *Kare wa dokushin desu.*
  I'm s. (spoken by a man) *Mada dokushin desu.*

I'm s. (spoken by a woman) *Mada mikon desu.*
  Is he s.? *Kare wa dokushin desu ka?*
  Is she s.? *Kanojo wa mikon desu ka?*
  She's s. *Kanojo wa mikon desu.*
single bed *shinguru-beddo*
single room (in a hotel) *shinguru rūmu*
sink: bathroom s. *semmendai*
  kitchen s. *nagashi*
sister (his, her, your older) *o-nēsan*
  (his, her, your younger) *imōtosan*
  (my older) *ane*
  (my younger) *imōto*
sister-in-law (his, her, your older) *giri-no-o-nēsan*
  (his, her, your younger) *giri-no-imōtosan*
  (my older) *ane*
  (my younger) *imōto*
Sit down, please. (on a chair) *Dōzo o-kake kudasai.*
Sit down, please. (on a cushion) *Dōzo o-suwari*

kudasai.

sitter (for children) *komori*

six (items) *muttsu* (see also p. 163, Numbers and Counting)

size (of clothes) *saizu*

extra-large s. *tokudai*

I take s. .... *Watashi no saizu wa ... desu.*

large s. *dai* (or *L*)

medium s. *chū* (or *M*)

small s. *shō* (or *S*)

What s. is it? *Kono saizu wa ikutsu desu ka?*

skates: ice s. *aisu-sukēto*

roller s. *rōrā-sukēto*

skating rink *sukēto-jō*

ski *sukī*

ski binding *sukī no shimegu*

ski lift *sukī-rifuto*

skim milk *dasshi-miruku*

skimpy *kechi na*

skin *kawa*

skin diving *sukin-daibingu*

ski resort *sukī-jō*

skirt *sukāto*

skyscraper *matenrō*

slacks *surakkusu*

slang *surangu*

sled *sori*

sleep: I couldn't s. last

night. *Yūbe nemurena-katta no desu.*

sleeping bag *surīpingu-bag-gu*

sleeping car (RR) *shindai-sha*

sleeping pill *suimin-yaku*

Sleep well! *Yoku o-yasumi nasai!*

sleepy *nemui*

Are you s.? *Nemui desu ka?*

I'm not s. *Nemuku ari-masen.*

I'm s. *Nemui desu.*

sleeve *sode*

half-s. *han-sode*

sleeveless *sode-nashi*

slender *hosoi*

slice (a) *hitokire*

slice of bread *pan hitokire*

slide (photo) *suraido*

sliding door *fusuma*

slim *hosoi*

slip (undergarment) *surippu*

Is my s. showing? *Surippu ga miete imasu ka?*

Your s. is showing. *Surip-pu ga miete imasu.*

slip: Don't s.! *Suberanai yō ni!*

That was a s. of the

tongue. *Kuchi o subera-shimashita.*

slipcover *isu-kabā*

slipper *surippā*

slippery *subesube shita*

sloppy *darashinai*

slot machine *surotto-ma-shin*

slow *osoi*

My watch is s. *Watashi no tokei wa okurete imasu.*

This train is s., isn't it? *Kono kisha wa noroi desu, ne?*

Your watch is s. *Anata no tokei wa okurete imasu.*

slower: Drive s., please. *Motto yukkuri hashitte kudasai.*

slowly *osoku*

Speak more s., please. *Motto yukkuri hanashite kudasai.*

slow-motion *surō-mōshon*

slum *himmingai*

slush (soft snow) *yuki-doke*

small *chiisai*

too s. *chiisa-sugimasu*

small change *komakai kane*

small slam (bridge) *sumō-ru-suramu*

smart (intelligent) *rikō na*

smell (odor) *nioi*

I s. smoke. *Kemuri no nioi ga shimasu.*

Something s. bad. *Nani ka kusai nioi ga shimasu.*

Something s. good. *Nani ka ii nioi ga shimasu.*

smile (a) *hohoemi*

smoke: Do you mind if I s.? *Tabako o sutte mo ii desu ka?*

smoke (vapor) *kemuri*

I smell s. *Kemuri no nioi ga shimasu.*

smoky *kemutai*

smooth *nameraka na*

snack *sunakku*

afternoon s. *o-yatsu*

snake *hebi*

snakeskin *hebigawa*

snap (on clothing) *sunappu*

snapshot *sunappu*

sneakers *undō-gutsu*

sneeze (a) *kushami*

snorkel *sunōkeru*

snow (the) *yuki*

snow: Do you think it's going to s.? *Yuki ga furu deshō ka?*

I don't think it's going to

s. *Yuki wa furanai deshō.*

I think it's going to s. *Yuki ga furu deshō.*

snowball *yukidama*

snowflake *yuki no kesshō*

snowing: Has it stopped s.? *Yuki wa yamimashita ka?*

Is it s.? *Yuki ga futte imasu ka?*

It's stopped s. *Yuki ga yamimashita.*

It's not s. *Yuki wa futte imasen.*

It's s. *Yuki ga futte imasu.*

snowman *yuki-daruma*

snowplow *josetsuki*

snowstorm *fubuki*

snowsuit (coverall for children) *kābā-ōru*

snug *kojimmari to shita*

so: Do you think s.? *Sō omoimasu ka?*

Is that s.? *Sō desu ka?*

I don't think s. *Sō omoimasen.*

I don't think s. either. *Watashi mo sō omoimasen.*

I think s. *Sō omoimasu.*

So am I. *Watashi mo sō desu.*

soap *sekken*

a cake of s. *sekken ikko*

soap dish *sekken-bako*

soap flakes *sentaku-sekken*

soap powder *kona-sekken*

soapsuds *sekken no awa*

sober (temperate) *osake o hikaeteiru*

sock *kutsushita*

socket wrench *soketto-renchi*

soda: baking s. (bicarbonate) *jūsō*

ice cream s. *aisu-kurīmu sōda*

soda (water) *sōdasui*

sofa bed *sofā-beddo*

soft *yawarakai*

soft-boiled egg *hanjuku-tamago*

soft drink (non-carbonated) *jūsu*

softly *yawarakaku*

soil (earth) *tsuchi*

soiled *kitanai*

sold *ureta*

soldier *heitai*

sold out *uri-kire*

sole (shoe) *kutsu-zoko*

solitaire (card game) *hitori-torampu*

some *ikura ka*

somebody *dare ka*

someday *itsuka*

somehow *dō ni ka*

someone *dare ka*

something *nani ka*

Something smells bad. *Nani ka kusai nioi ga shimasu.*

Something smells good. *Nani ka ii nioi ga shimasu.*

Something's the matter. *Nani ka arimashita, ne.*

Something's wrong. *Nani ka arimashita, ne.*

sometime *itsu ka*

Come and see me s. *Itsuka asobi ni irasshai.*

sometimes *toki-doki*

somewhere *doko ka*

son (his, her, your) *musuko-san*

(my) *musuko*

song *uta*

son-in-law (his, her, your) *o-mukosan*

(my) *muko*

soon *sugu*

Are you coming back s.? *Sugu o-kaeri ni narimasu ka?*

How s. can you do it? *Dono gurai hayaku deki-masu ka?*

How s. will it be ready? *Donokurai de dekimasu ka?*

I'll be back s. *Sugu kaerimasu.*

sore (a) *kaiyō*

sore: Is it s.? *Itai desu ka?*

It's not s. *Itaku arimasen.*

It's s. *Itai desu.*

sore throat *intōtsū*

Do you have a s. t.? *Nodo ga itai desu ka?*

I have a s. t. *Nodo ga itai desu.*

sorry: I'm s. (Excuse me.) *Gomen nasai.*

I'm s. (I regret your misfortune.) *Zannen de-su.*

I'm s. to have kept you waiting. *O-machidō-sa-ma.*

I feel s. for you. *O-kino-doku-sama.*

soul *tamashii*

sound (a) *oto*
soup (J.) *suimono*
soup (W.) *sūpu*
  a bowl of s. *sūpu ippai*
  beef bouillon *bīfu-buiyon*
  chicken s. *chikin-sūpu*
  pea s. *mame-sūpu*
  tomato s. *tomato-sūpu*
  vegetable s. *yasai-sūpu*
soup bowl *sūpu-zara*
soup spoon *sūpu-supūn*
sour *suppai*
south *minami*
Southeast Asia *Tōnan Ajia*
souvenir *o-miyage*
  I brought you a s. *O-miya-ge o motte kite imasu.*
Soviet Russia *Soren*
soy sauce *o-shōyu*
spa *onsen*
spade (card) *supēdo*
spaghetti *supagetti*
spaghetti with meat sauce *supagetti-mīto-sōsu*
spanking *hirate-uchi*
spare time *hima*
spare tire *supeā-taiya*
sparkling wine *awadachi-wain*
spark plug *supāku-pura-gu*

sparrow *suzume* ⌈*naifu*
spatula (for butter) *batā-*
speak: Do you s. English? *Eigo o hanashimasu ka?*
speaker (for recorder) *supī-kā*
Speak more clearly (slow-ly), please. *Motto hak-kiri (yukkuri) hanashi-te kudasai.*
special *tokubetsu na*
special-delivery letter *so-kutatsu*
speed limit *supīdo-seigen* (see also p. 172, Speed Table)
speedometer *supīdomētā*
spice *kōryō*
spill: Don't s. it! *Kobosanai yō ni!*
spinach *hōrensō*
spine *sebone*
splint *soegi*
splinter *toge*
spoiled (rotten) *kusatta*
spoiled child *dadakko*
sponge *kaimen*
sponge cake (J.) *kasutera*
spool of thread *ito hitomaki*
spoon: *supūn*
  soup s. *sūpu-supūn*

sugar s. *satō-supūn*
tables. *tēburu-supūn*
tables. (measuring) *ō-saji*
teas. *tī-supūn*
teas. (measuring) *ko-saji*
sport *supōtsu*
sporting-goods store *undōguya*
sports car *supōtsu-kā*
sports event (school, etc.) *undōkai*
sport shirt *supōtsu-shatsu*
sports jacket *supōtsu-jaketto*
sports match *shiai*
sportswear *supōtsu-ueā*
spot *shimi*
spot remover *shimi-nuki*
sprain *nenza*
sprained ankle: I have a s. a. *Ashikubi o nenza shimashita.*
spray (off the water) *shibuki*
sprayer (for houseplants) *jōro*
spray starch *supurē-sutāchi*
spring (season) *haru*
springtime *haru*
spring vacation *haru-yasumi*
square (shape) *shikaku*
squash (vegetable) *kabocha*

squeeze: a tight s. *kiki-ippatsu*
squeezer (for lemons) *remon-shibori*
squid *ika*
stadium *sutajiamu*
stage (elevated platform) *butai*
stain *yogore*
stained *yogoreta*
stainless steel *sutenresu*
stairs *kaidan*
stairway *kaidan*
stale *furui*
stale bread *furui pan*
stamp: airmail s. *kōkū-kitte*
postage s. *kitte*
standing room (theater) *tachimi-seki*
Stand up! *Tatte kudasai!*
Stand up straight! *Massugu tatte kudasai!*
star *hoshi*
star (films, etc.) *sutā*
starch *sutāchi*
spray s. *supurē-sutāchi*
start: When does it (the train) s.? *Nanji ni demasu ka?*
When does it (the play) s.? *Nanji ni hajimarimasu*

ka?

starter (car) *sutātā*

stateroom (on a ship) *sen-shitsu*

station: radio s. *hōsōkyoku*
railroad s. *eki*

stationary *seishi shita*

stationery *bumbōgu*

stationery store *bumbōguten*

stationmaster *ekichō*

station platform (RR) *hōmu*

steak *sutēki*

steam iron *jōki-airon*

steamship *kisen*

steel wool *kanedawashi*

steep *kyū na*

steering wheel *handoru*

step (of a stair) *dan*

step: Watch your s.! *Ashi-moto ni ki o tsukete kudasai!*

stepladder *kyatatsu*

sterile *mukin no*

sterling silver *jungin*

stern (of a ship) *sembi*

stew (meat & vegetables) *shichū*

steward (on a ship) *suchu-wādo*

stewardess (on an airplane) *suchuwādesu*

stewed fruit *nikomi-furūtsu*

stick (a) *bō*

stiff *kowabatta*

stiff neck: I have a s. n. *Kubi o nechigaemashita.*

stillborn child *shizanji*

stings: That s. *Sore wa shi-mimasu.*

stir: Don't s. it. *Mazenai yō ni.*

Stir it, please. *Mazete ku-dasai.*

stirrup *abumi*

stock (securities) *kabu*
common s. *ippan-kabu*
preferred s. *yūsen-kabu*

stockbroker *kabu-nakagai-nin*

stock exchange *kabushiki-torihikijō*

stockholder *kabunushi*

stockings *kutsushita*
a pair of s. *kutsushita issoku*

stole: fur s. *kegawa-sutōru*

stomach *o-naka*

stomach ache: Do you have a s. a.? *O-naka ga itai desu ka?*
I have a s. a. *O-naka ga itai desu.*

stone *ishi*
stone lantern *ishi-dōrō*
stone wall *ishi-bei*
stool (seat) *koshikake*
Stop here! *Koko de ii desu!*
Stop it! *Yoshinasai!*
stoplight *teishi shingō*
stopper (sink, etc.) *sen*
storage battery *chikudenchi*
store (shop) *mise*
store window *shō-uindō*
storm *arashi*
    rains. *arashi*
    snows. *fubuki*
    thunders. *rai-u*
storm window *nijū-mado*
story (narrative) *o-hanashi*
story (floor) *kai*
    one-s. house *hiraya*
    two-s. house *nikaiya*
stove: kitchen s. *gasu-renji*
straight *massugu na*
straight (without diluent) *sutorēto*
straight ahead *massugu saki ni*
    Go s. a.! *Massugu itte kudasai!*
straight hair *massugu na kami*
straight pin *machi-bari*

strainer *ura-goshi*
    tea s. *cha-koshi*
strange *hen na*
stranger *shiranai hito*
straw *wara*
straw (for sipping) *sutorō*
strawberry *ichigo*
strawberry shortcake *ichi-go-shōtokēki*
straw mat *tatami*
stream *ogawa*
streamer: carp s. *koi-nobori*
street *tōri*
    dead-end s. *fukuro-kōji*
    one-way s. *ippō-tsūkō*
streetcar *densha*
street corner *kado*
strength *chikara*
strict *genkaku na*
strike (labor) *sutoraiki*
strike (in baseball) *sutoraiku*
string *himo*
string beans *saya-ingen*
stroke (medical) *sotchū*
stroller (baby carriage) *uba-guruma*
strong *tsuyoi*
strong (of coffee) *koi*
stubborn: *gōjō na*
    Don't be s.! *Gōjō o harazu ni!*

student (general) *seito*, (university) *gakusei*

study (room) *shosai*

stuffing (for poultry) *tsume-mono*

stupid *baka na*

sty (eye infection) *monomorai*

style *sutairu*

stylish *sumāto na*

subscription (to a magazine, paper, etc.) *yoyaku*

subtle *kōmyō na*

suburb *kōgai*

subway *chikatetsu*

sucker (lollipop) *bōtsuki-ame*

suddenly *kyū ni*

sugar *o-satō*

a cup (measuring) of s. *o-satō ichikappu*

brown s. *aka-zatō*

powdered s. *kona-zatō*

sugar bowl *satō-ire*

sugar spoon *satō-supūn*

suggestion *teian*

suit (man's) *sebiro*, (woman's) *sūtsu*

suitcase *toranku*

suit coat *uwagi*

suits: It s. you well. *Anata ni ni-aimasu.*

summer *natsu*

summer resort *hishochi*

summertime *natsu*

summer vacation *natsu-yasumi*

sun: Is the s. out? *Hi ga dete imasu ka?*

The s. is out. *Hi ga dete imasu.*

sunbath *nikkōyoku*

sunburned: You're s. *Yake-mashita, ne.*

sundae (ice cream) *kurīmu-sandē*

Sunday *Nichiyōbi*

Sunday school *Nichiyō-gakkō*

sunglasses *sangarasu*

sunlamp *taiyōtō*

sunlight *nikkō*

sunrise *hinode*

sunset *hinoiri*

sunshade (parasol) *higasa*

sunshine *nikkō*

suntan *hiyake*

suntan oil *hiyake-oiru*

superiority complex *yūe-tsukan*

supermarket *sūpā-māketto*

supernatural *chōshizenteki na*

superstition *meishin*

superstitious *meishin-bukai*

supervisor *kantoku*

supper *bangohan*

suppose: I s. so. *Sō ka mo shiremasen.*

  I s. not. *Sō de wa nai ka mo shiremasen.*

Sure! *Mochiron!*

sure: Are you s.? *Tashika desu ka?*

  Don't be too s. *Sonna ni hakkiri ienai deshō.*

  I'm not s. *Tashika de wa arimasen.*

  I'm s. *Tashika desu.*

surf *yose-nami*

surfboard *sāfubōdo*

surfing *sāfin*

surgeon *geka-i*

surgery (operation) *shujutsu*

surname *myōji*

surprised: I'm not s. *Odoroite imasen.*

  I'm s. *Odorokimashita.*

  I'm s. to see you. *Omoigakemasen deshita.*

  I wouldn't be s. *Sō darō to omoimasu.*

swallow (bird) *tsubame*

swatter *hae-tataki*

sweat *ase*

sweater *sētā*

  (cardigan) *kādegan*

  (pullover) *sētā*

sweat shirt *torēnā*

sweeper: carpet s. *kāpetto-sōjiki*

sweet *amai*

  Is it s. enough? *Amasa wa jūbun desu ka?*

  It's not s. enough. *Amari amaku arimasen.*

  It's too s. *Ama-sugimasu.*

sweetheart *koibito*

sweet potato *satsuma-imo*

  baked s. p. *yaki-imo*

sweet roll *kashi-pan*

swim cap *kaisui-bō*

swimming pool *pūru*

swim suit *mizugi*

swim trunks *kaisui-pantsu*

swing (for children) *buranko*

swinging door *kaiten-doa*

Swiss cheese *Suisu-chīzu*

switch (electrical) *suitchi*

swollen: It's s. *Harete kite imasu.*

sympathetic *yasashii*

  He (she) is s. *Kare (kanojo) wa yasashii desu.*

sympathize: I s. with you.

Anata ni dōjō shimasu.
sympathy: Please accept my s. *Go-dōjō mōshiagemasu.*

symphony orchestra *kangen-gakudan*
syringe *senjōki*
syrup *shiroppu*

T

table *tēburu*
all-purpose t. (J.) *tsukue*
card t. (J.) *torampu-tēburu*
coffee t. *kōhī-tēburu*
dining t. *shokutaku*
eating t. (J.) *chabudai*
end t. *wakitēburu*
kitchen t. *kichin-tēburu*
night t. *beddo no wakitēburu*
tablecloth *tēburu-kurosu*
table lamp *takujō-sutando*
table leaf (extender) *tēburu-hamekomibu*
tablespoon *tēburu-supūn*
tablespoon (measuring) *ō-saji*
a t. of ... *ō-saji ippai*
tablet (pill) *jōzai*
tack *byō*
thumbt. *gabyō*

tail *shippo*
taillight (car) *tēru-rampu*
tailor *yōfukuya-san*
tailor-made *tērā-mēdo*
tailor shop *yōfukuya* (*see also* p. 150, At the Dressmaker or Tailor Shop)
tailpipe *tēru-paipu*
tails (formal dress for men) *embifuku*
take: Don't t. it! *Sore o totte wa ikemasen!*
May I t. this? *Kore o itadakemasu ka?*
Take it. *Dōzo o-tori kudasai.*
Take it back. *Sore o kaeshite kudasai.*
Take it off. *Sore o nuginasai.*
takeoff (airplane) *ririku*
Take some, please. *Dōzo*

o-tori kudasai.
tale monogatari
talk (a) o-hanashi
tall sei no takai
 How t. are you? *Anata no
  sei wa dono gurai desu
  ka?*
tally (bridge) aifuda
tame nareta
tangerine mikan
tape: adhesive t. bansōkō
 friction t. zetsuen-tēpu
 masking t. hōsōyō-tēpu
 recording t. rokuon-tēpu
 scotch t. sero-tēpu
tape measure makijaku
tape recorder tēpu-rekōdā
tapioca tapioka
tart (small pie) taruto
tart (sour) suppai
taste (of food) aji
taste: in bad t. gebita
 in good t. kōshō na
tasteless ajike-nai
tasty oishii
tax zei
 business t. eigyōzei
 city t. shiminzei
 customs t. kanzei
 income t. shotokuzei
 ward t. kuminzei

tax charge zeikin
tax-exempt menzei no
tax-free menzei no
tax office zeimusho
taxi takushī
 Call me a t., please. *Takushī o yonde kudasai. (see
  also p. 147, Instructions
  to a Taxi Driver)*
taxi driver takushī no untenshu
tea: a cup of t. (J.) o-cha
 ippai, (W.) kōcha ippai
 black t. kōcha
 black t. with lemon remon-
  tī
 green t. o-cha
 iced t. aisu-tī
tea bag tī-baggu
tea ceremony chanoyu
teacher sensei
teacup (J.) chawan; yunomi
teacup (W.) kōcha-jawan
teahouse (J.) chaya
teakettle yakan
teapot (J.) kyūsu, (W.) tī-potto
tear (eye lubricant) namida
tear: Don't t. it! *Yabutte
 wa ikemasen!*
 Don't t. it up! *Yabutte*

shimatte wa ikemasen!
T. it up! *Yabutte oite kudasai!*

tearoom (coffee shop) *kissaten*

tease: Don't t. *Ijimenai de kudasai.*

tea shop *o-chaya*

teaspoon *tī-supūn*

teaspoon (measuring) *kosaji*
a t. of ... *kosaji-ippai*

tea strainer *cha-koshi*

tea whisk (J.) *chasen*

tedious *taikutsu na*

tee *tī*

teenager *jūdai no hito*

teeth *ha*

telegram *dempō*
Where can I send a t.? *Dempō o doko de dasemasu ka?*

telegraph office *denshin-kyoku*

telephone *denwa*
May I use the t.? *Denwa o kashite kudasai.*
Where can I find a t.? *Denwa wa doko ni arimasu ka?* (*see also* p. 155, Telephoning)

Telephone! (for you) *O-denwa desu!*

telephone booth *denwa-shitsu*

telephone call *denwa*
long-distance call *chōkyori-denwa*
overseas call *kokusai-denwa*

telephone directory *denwa-chō*

Telephone me, please. *Denwa o kudasai.*

telephone number *denwa-bangō*

telephone operator *kōkan-shu*

telephone receiver *juwaki*

television *terebi*

temperature (air, water, etc.) *ondo*
What's the t. outside? *Soto no ondo wa nando desu ka?* (*see also* p. 171, Temperature Table)

temperature (body) *taion*
Does he (she) have a t.? *Kare (kanojo) wa netsu ga arimasu ka?*
Do you have a t.? *Anata wa netsu ga arimasu ka?*

I don't have a t. *Watashi wa netsu ga arimasen.*

I have a t. *Netsu ga arimasu.*

Take my t., please. *Netsu o hakatte kudasai.*

tempered: bad-t. *iji no warui*

  good-t. *yasashii*

  quick-t. *okorippoi*

temple (Buddhist) *o-tera*

temporary *kari no*

temporary job *tōza no shigoto*

tempura oil (for cooking) *tempura-abura*

ten (items) *tō* (*see also p. 163, Numbers and Counting*)

tenant *shakuyanin*

tender (of meat) *yawarakai*

tenderloin (beef) *gyū-hireniku*

tennis *tenisu*

tennis ball *tenisu-bōru*

tennis court *tenisu-kōto*

tennis match *tenisu no shi-*

tennis racket *raketto* ⌊*ai*

tennis shoes *undō-gutsu*

tense *kinchō shita*

ten thousand *ichiman*

term (school) *gakki*

terminal (airline building) *eā-tāminaru*

termite *shiro-ari*

terrace *terasu*

test *shiken*

Thanks! *Dōmo!*

Thanksgiving *Kanshasai*

Thank you. (in general) *Arigatō gozaimasu.*

  (for ordinary services) *Go-kurō-sama.*

  (to someone who has gone out of his way) *O-sewa-sama deshita.*

  (for the meal, drinks, etc.) *Go-chisōsama deshita.*

that *sono*

thatched roof *kayabuki-yane*

That's a good idea. *Sore wa ii kangae desu.*

That's enough. *Sore de kekkō desu.*

That's interesting! *Sore wa omoshiroi desu!*

That's right. *Sō desu.*

That's understood. *Wakarimashita.*

That's wonderful! *Sore wa subarashii desu!*

That's wrong. *Sore wa chigaimasu.*

that one *sore*

that way (in that direction) *achira e*

(in that manner) *sō*

thawed *toketa*

theater (for plays) *gekijō*

theater (for films) *eigakan*

theater ticket *gekijō-nyū-jōken*

their *karera no*

them *karera o*

for (to) t. *karera ni*

there *asoko*

over t. *achira*

There he (she) is. *Asoko ni imasu.*

thermometer *kandankei*

clinical t. *taionki*

thermos (bottle or jug) *mahōbin*

thermostat *sāmosutatto*

they *karera wa (ga)*

thick (of flat things) *atsui,* e.g., a thick book *atsui hon*

(of round things) *futoi,* e.g., thick legs *futoi ashi*

(of liquids, colors, hair, etc.) *koi,* e.g., thick coffee *koi kōhī*

thief *dorobō*

Thief! *Dorobō da!*

thigh *futomomo*

thimble *yubinuki*

thin (of flat things, colors, liquids) *usui,* e.g., a thin color *usui iro*

(of round things) *hosoi,* e.g., thin legs *hosoi ashi*

(of persons) *yaseta,* e.g., a thin man *yaseta otoko*

(sparse) *mabara no*

thinner: You're getting t. *Yasemashita, ne.*

thing *mono*

think: Do you t. so? *Sō omoimasu ka?*

I don't t. so. *Sō omoimasen.*

I don't t. so, either. *Watashi mo sō omoimasen.*

I t. so. *Sō omoimasu.*

What do you t. (about it)? *Anata wa dō omoimasu ka?*

third (the) *dai-san*

one t. *sambun-no-ichi*

thirsty: Are you t.? *Nodo ga kawaite imasu ka?*

I'm not t. *Nodo wa kawaite imasen.*

I'm t. *Nodo ga kawaki-mashita.*

this *kono*

this afternoon *kyō no gogo*

this evening *komban*

this month *kongetsu*

this morning *kesa*

this noon *kyō no hiru*

this one *kore*

this time *kondo*

this way (in this direction) *kochira e*

(in this manner) *kō*

this week *konshū*

this year *kotoshi*

thorough *mattaku no*

thoroughbred (horse) *sara-bureddo*

thoroughly *tetteiteki ni*

thought (a) *kangae*

thoughtful *omoiyari no aru*

thoughtless *omoiyari no nai*

thousand (one) *sen*

ten t. *ichiman*

thread *ito*

a spool of t. *ito hitomaki*

three (items) *mittsu* (see also p. 163, Numbers and Counting)

three quarters *yombun-no-san*

three times a day *ichinichi ni sando*

throat *nodo*

Do you have a sore t.? *Nodo ga itai desu ka?*

I have a sore t. *Nodo ga itai desu.*

sore t. *intōtsū*

through (by way of, by means of, etc.) ... *o tōshite*

through (finished): Are you t.? *Sumimashita ka?*

I'm not t. *Sunde imasen.*

I'm t. *Sumimashita.*

throw away: Don't throw it away. *Sutenai yō ni.*

I'm going to throw it away. *Kore o sutemasu.*

Throw this away, please. *Sutete kudasai.*

thumb *oyayubi*

thumbtack *gabyō*

thunder *kaminari*

thunder & lightning *ina-bikari*

thunderclap *rakurai*

thunderstorm *rai-u*

Thursday *Mokuyōbi*

thyroid *kōjōsen*

ticket (train & plane) *kippu*
  express-train t. (long-distance) *kyūkōken*
  1st-class t. *ittō jōshaken*
  2nd-class t. *nitō jōshaken*
  one-way t. *katamichi kippu*
  ordinary-train t. (long-distance) *jōshaken*
  platform t. *nyūjōken*
  round-trip t. *ōfuku kippu*
  season t. *teiki*
  sleeper t. *shindaiken*
  special-express-train t. (long-distance) *tokkyū ken*
ticket (admission) *nyūjōken*
ticket (traffic violation) *kōtsū-ihan shōkanjō*
ticket window *mado-guchi*
tide: high t. *manchō*
  low t. *kanchō*
tight (clothing) *kyukutsu na*
  (stingy) *kechi na*
  (tipsy) *chidori-ashi no*
tile (roof) *kawara*
time: all the t. *itsu mo*
  a long t. *nagaku*
  a long t. ago *zutto mae*
  a short t. *mijikai aida*
  a short t. ago *sukoshi mae*
  at any t. *itsu de mo*

at the present t. *ima wa*
at the same t. *dōji ni*
Do you have t.? *Jikan ga arimasu ka?*
each t. *mai-do*
every t. ... *tambi ni*
free (leisure) t. *hima*
from t. to t. *toki-doki*
How much t. do I (you, we) have? *Dono gurai jikan ga arimasu ka?*
I (you, we) don't have t. *Jikan ga arimasen.*
Is there t.? *Jikan ga arimasu ka?*
last t. *kono mae*
next t. *tsugi ni*
old-t. *mukashi no*
Once upon a t. *Mukashi, mukashi*
on t. *jikan-dōri ni*
some other t. *ato de*
sometime *itsu ka*
Take your t. *Go-yukkuri.*
There isn't much t. *Jikan ga amari nai.*
There's plenty of t. *Mada takusan jikan ga arimasu.*
this t. *kondo*
What t. is it? *Nanji desu*

ka? (see also p. 167,
Telling Time) ⌜tsu
time exposure taimu roshu-
times: many t. tabi-tabi
  modern t. gendai
  old t. mukashi
  several t. nankai ka
  somet. toki-doki
Time's up. Jikan desu.
timetable jikokuhyō
tin can (filled with food)
  kanzume, (empty) aki-
  kan
tin foil suzu-haku
tiny chiisa na
tip (gratuity) chippu
tire taiya
  flat t. panku
  spare t. supeā-taiya
  tubeless t. chūburesu-taiya
tired: Aren't you t.? Tsukarete imasen ka?
  Are you t.? Tsukarema-
  shita ka?
  I'm not t. Tsukarete imasen.
  I'm t. Tsukarete imasu.
tire pump kūki-ire
tissue paper chirigami
toast tōsuto
  a slice of t. tōsuto hitokire

toaster tōsutā
tobacco tabako
tobacco pouch kizami-ta-
  bako-ire
today kyō
toe ashi no yubi
toenail ashi no tsume
toenail scissors tsume-kiri-
together issho ni ⌊basami
  all t. minna de
to her kanojo ni
to him kare ni
toilet o-te-arai
  flush t. suisen benjo
  public t. kyōdō-benjo
toilet cleaner (man with
  pump truck) kumitoriya
toilet paper (W.) toiretto-
  pēpā, (J.) chirigami
toll road yūryō-dōro
tomato tomato
  a can of t. tomato hitokan
tomato juice tomato-jūsu
tomato soup tomato-sūpu
tombstone hakaishi
to me watashi ni
tomorrow ashita
  day after t. asatte
  I'll see you t. Mata ashita.
tomorrow afternoon ashita
  no gogo

tomorrow evening *ashita no ban*

tomorrow morning *ashita no asa*

tomorrow night *myōban*

tomorrow noon *ashita no hiru*

ton (metric) *ton*

tongue *shita*

tongue (language) *kotoba*

tongue-tied *shita no mawaranai*

tonight (all night) *komban*

tonight (this evening) *komban*

tonsillectomy *hentōsen tekishutsu-jutsu*

tonsillitis *hentōsen-en*

tonsils *hentōsen*

too (also) *... mo*

too (more than) *...-sugimasu*

too bad: That's too b. *O-kinodoku-sama desu.*

too big *ōki-sugimasu*

tool *dōgu*

too little (amount) *fuzoku*

tool kit *dōgu-bako*

too many *ō-sugimasu*

too much *ō-sugimasu*

too small *chiisa-sugimasu*

tooth *ha*

toothache *ha-ita*

Do you have a t.? *Ha ga itai desu ka?*

I have a t. *Ha ga itai desu.*

toothbrush *ha-burashi*

toothpaste *ha-migaki*

toothpick *tsumayōji*

tooth powder *ha-migakiko*

top (peak) *chōjō*

top (the) *ue*

on t. of ... *no ue ni*

top (toy) *koma*

torn *yabureta*

tossed green salad *gurīn-sarada*

total *gōkei*

to them *karera ni*

touch: Don't t. it! *Sawatte wa ikemasen!*

tough *katai*

tour *ryokō*

tour bus *kankō-basu*

tour guide *ryokō-gaido*

tourist *kankōkyaku*

to us *watashitachi ni*

towel *taoru*

bath t. *basu-taoru*

dish t. *fukin*

hand t. *tenugui*

hot t. *o-shibori*

kitchen t. *kichin-taoru*

towel rack *taoru-kake*
town *machi*
tow truck *ken·insha*
toy *omocha*
to you (singular) *anata ni*
    (plural) *anatagata ni*
toy shop *omochaya*
track: racet. (horse) *keibajō*
    railroad t. *senro*
    Which t. does the train
    leave from? *Kisha wa
    nambansen desu ka?*
track number ... *-bansen*
trade union *rōdō-kumiai*
traffic *kōtsū*
    one-way t. *ippō-tsūkō*
traffic circle *rōtarī*
traffic jam *kōtsū-jūtai*
traffic light *kōtsū-shingō*
traffic ticket (summons) *kō-
    tsū-ihan shōkanjō*
tragedy *higeki*
train: express t. *kyūkō*
    freight t. *kamotsu-ressha*
    local t. *futsū-ressha*
    railroad t. (steam), *kisha*
    (electric) *densha*
    special express t. *tokkyū*
train conductor *shashō*
train schedule *ressha-daiya*
train seat *ressha no zaseki*

train track *senro*
transistor radio *toranjisu-
    tā-rajio*
translator *hon·yakusha*
trash (refuse) *kuzu*
travel agency *kōtsū-kōsha*
traveler's check *toraberā-
    chekku*
tray *o-bon*
tree *ki*
trellis *kōshidana*
triangle *sankaku*
trick (bridge) *torikku*
tricycle *sanrinsha*
trio (instrumental) *sanjūsō*
trip (journey) *ryokō*
trip: Don't t.! *Tsumazuka-
    nai yō ni!*
triple *sambai no*
trivet *shikidai; gotoku*
tropical fish *nettaigyo*
tropics *nettai*
trouble *shimpai*
    What's the t.? *Dō shima-
    shita ka?*
trousers *zubon*
    a pair of t. *zubon ippon*
trousseau *yomeiri ishō*
trout *masu*
    rainbow t. *niji-masu*
truck *torakku*

delivery t. *umpansha*
dump t. *dampu-kā*
tow t. *ken·insha*
truck driver *torakku no untenshu*
true: Isn't that t.? *Hontō desu, ne?*
Is that t.? *Hontō desu ka?*
That's not t. *Sore wa chigaimasu.*
That's t. *Hontō desu, yo.*
trump (bridge) *kirifuda*
trunk (of a tree) *miki*
trunk (luggage) *toranku*
car t. *toranku*
trunk lid (car) *toranku no futa*
truth *hontō no koto*
It's the t. *Hontō desu yo.*
truthful *shinjitsu no*
try: I'll t. *Yatte mimasu.*
I'll t. it. *Yatte mimasu.*
Will you t. it? *Yatte mimasen ka?*
Try it on. (coats, dresses, jackets, shirts) *Kite mite kudasai.*
(hats, wigs) *Kabutte mite kudasai.*
(shoes, socks, trousers) *Haite mite kudasai.*

(gloves, rings, wristwatches) *Hamete mite kudasai.*
(earrings, brooches) *Tsukete mite kudasai.*
Try some. (food, etc.) *Hitotsu o-tori kudasai.*
Try to come early. *Hayaku irassharu yō ni shite kudasai.*
tub: batht. *furo-oke*
washt. *tarai*
tube (tire) *chūbu*
tubeless tire *chūburesu-taiya*
tuberculosis *kekkaku*
Tuesday *Kayōbi*
tuition *jugyōryō*
tuna fish *maguro*
tuna-fish salad *maguro sarada*
tuna-fish-salad sandwich *maguro-sarada sandoitchi*
tune: It's in t. *Oto ga atte imasu.*
It's out of t. *Oto ga kurutte imasu.*
tune-up (car) *chūnnappu*
tunnel *tonneru*
turkey *shichimenchō*
roast t. *rōsuto-tākī*

turn: It's my t. *Watashi no ban desu.*

It's your t. *Anata no ban desu.*

Whose t. is it? *Donata no ban desu ka?*

Turn around, please. *Ushiro o mukinasai.*

turn back: Let's t. b. *Modorimashō.*

Turn here. *Koko o magatte kudasai.*

turnip *kabu*

Turn it inside out. *Uragaeshite kudasai.*

Turn it upside-down. *Sakasama ni shite kudasai.*

Turn left. *Hidari e magatte kudasai.*

Turn off the light, please. *Denki o keshite kudasai.*

Turn off the water, please. *Suidō o shimete kudasai.*

Turn on the light, please. *Denki o tsukete kudasai.*

Turn on the water, please. *Suidō o akete kudasai.*

Turn right. *Migi e magatte kudasai.*

turn signal (car) *hōkō-shijiki*

turpentine *matsu-yani*

tuxedo *takishīdo*

TV announcer *anaunsā*

TV channel *channeru*

TV set *terebi*

tweed *tsuīdo*

tweezers *ke-nuki*

twice *nido*

twice a day *ichinichi ni nido*

twice a month *ikkagetsu ni nido*

twice a week *isshūkan ni nido*

twice a year *ichinen ni nido*

twilight *yūgata*

twin beds *tsuin-beddo*

twins *futago*

two (items) *futatsu* (see also p. 163, Numbers and Counting)

two-piece dress *tsūpīsu*

typewriter *taipuraitā*

typewriter ribbon *taipu-raitā-ribon*

typhoon *taifū*

typing paper *taipu-yōshi*

U

ugly *minikui*
ulcer (stomach) *ikaiyō*
umbrella (J.) *kasa*
  (W.) *kōmori-gasa*
umbrolla stand *kasa-tate*
unattractive *hitome o hika-nai*
unbleached *sarashite inai*
unbreakable *koware-nikui*
uncertain *fuan na*
uncle (his, her, your) *ojisan*
  (my) *oji*
uncomfortable *igokochi no warui*
unconscious *muishiki no*
  He (she) is u. *Ki o ushinai-mashita.*
uncooked *nama no*
undecided *kimaranai*
under ... *no shita ni*
underarm *waki-no-shita*
underbrush *yabu*
underclothes *shitagi*
underdone *nama-yake*

underexposed (film) *ro-shutsu-busoku*
undergraduate *gakusei*
underneath *shita no hō*
underpants *pantsu*
underpass *chikadō*
undershirt *shitagi*
undershorts *pantsu*
  a pair of u. *pantsu ichimai*
understand: Do you u.?
  Wakarimashita ka?
  Do you u. English? *Eigo ga wakarimasu ka?*
  I don't u. *Wakarimasen.*
  I don't u. Japanese. *Ni-hongo wa wakarimasen.*
  I u. *Wakarimasu.*
understood: That's u. *Wa-karimashita.*
understudy *daiyaku*
undertaker *sōgiya*
undertow *suiryū*
underwater *suichū*
underwear *shitagi*

underweight *mekata-busoku*

undone: It's come u. *Hazurete kimashita.*

undressed *hadaka no*

unemployed person *shitsugyōsha*

unemployment insurance *shitsugyō-hoken*

unequal *fubyōdō na*

uneven *dekoboko shita*
This hem is u. *Kono suso wa dekoboko shite imasu.*

unexpected *omoegakenai*

unfair *fukōhei na*

unfashionable *jidai-okure no*

unfortunate *fukō na*

unfortunately *ainiku*

unfrozen *reitō de nai*

unhappy *fukō na*
I'm u. *Watashi wa shiawase de wa arimasen.*

unhealthy *fukenkō na*

uniform (clothing) *seifuku*

unimportant: It's u. *Taishita koto de wa arimasen.*

uninteresting *tsumaranai*

unique *mata-to-nai*

United States of America *Amerika Gasshūkoku*

university *daigaku*

unkempt *kushi-kezuranai*

unkind *fushinsetsu na*

unlucky: I'm (you're) u. *Un ga yoku nai.*

unlucky break *ainiku no dekigoto*

unnecessary *fuyō na*

unoccupied *hima na*

unpleasant *tanoshiku nai*

unpopular *ninki no nai*

unrefined (common) *somatsu na*

unsafe *abunai*

unselfish *rikoshin no nai*

untidy *chirakashita*

unused *tsukatte inai*

unusual *ijō na*

up *ue ni*
Get up! *Okite kudasai!*
Stand u.! *Tatte kudasai!*
Time is u. *Jikan desu.*
Wake u.! *Me o samashinasai!*

Up? (to elevator operator) *Ue desu ka?* ⌈*bai-nin*

upholsterer *kagu seizō ham-*

upkeep *ijihi*

upper berth *jōdan*

upset: Don't be u. *Ochitsukinasai.*

upside-down *sakasama ni*
It's u.-d. *Sakasama desu.*
Turn it u.-d. *Sakasama ni shite kudasai.*
upstairs *nikai*
up-to-date *ichiban atarashii*
urgent *kinkyū no*
urinal *shōbenjo*
urine *o-shikko*
us *watashitachi o*
for (to) u. *watashitachi ni*
use: It's no u. *Dame desu.*
What's the u.? *Shikata ga nai.*
use: Don't u. it. *Sore o tsukawanai de kudasai.*

May I u. this? *Kore o tsukatte mo ii desu ka?*
You may u. this. *Kore o tsukatte mo ii desu.*
used car *chūkosha*
useful *yaku ni tatsu*
Use it up. *Tsukatte shimatte kudasai.*
useless *dame na*
Use this. *Kore o tsukatte kudasai.*
usherette (theater) *annainin*
usually *taigai*
utensils *shokki*
writing u. *bumbōgu*
U-turn *yū-tān*

V

vacancy (room for rent) *akishitsu*
job v. *shūshokuguchi*
vacant: Is this seat v.? *Kono seki wa aite imasu ka?*
This seat is v. *Aite imasu.*
vacation *kyūka*
Christmas v. *Kurisumasu-kyūka*

spring v. *haru-yasumi*
summer v. *natsu-yasumi*
vaccination *shutō*
vacuum cleaner *denki-sōjiki*
valley *tani*
valuable *kichō na*
valuables *kichōhin*
valve (car) *barubu*

vanilla (extract) *banira*

vanilla ice cream *banira aisu-kurīmu*

varicose veins *jōmyaku-ryū*

vase *kabin*

veal *ko-ushi no niku*

veal chop *bīru choppu*

veal cutlet *ko-ushi katsure-tsu*

veal roast *rōsuto-bīru*

vegetable *yasai*

vegetable soup *yasai-sūpu*

vegetarian *saishoku-shugi-sha*

vein *ao-suji*

velvet *berubetto; birōdo*

velveteen *betchin*

Venetian blind *ita-sudare*

vent *tsūfūkō*

vertical *tate no*

very *taihen*

Very good! *Taihen ii desu!*

vest *chokki*

vestibule *genkan*

veterinary *jū-i*

vice versa *gyaku ni*

view *keshiki*

villa *bessō*

village *mura*

vinegar *su*

violet (flower) *sumire*

virgin *ki-musume*

visa *biza*

visitor *hōmonsha*

vitamin pills *bitamin-jōzai*

vitamins *bitamin*

vocalist *kashu*

vodka *uokka*

voice *koe*

in a loud v. *ōkii koe de*

in a low v. *chiisai koe de*

volcano *kazan*

volley ball *barē-bōru*

vomited: I (he, she) vomited. *Hakimashita.*

vomiting *ōto*

vomitive (emetic) *tozai*

vulgar *gehin na*

W

wad (a) *katamari*
waffle *waffuru*
waffle iron *waffuru-yaki*
wages *chingin*
waist *koshi*
Wait! *Matte kudasai!*
Wait a minute! *Chotto matte kudasai!*
waiter *kyūji*
head. w. *chīfu-uētā*
Waiter! (Waitress!) *Chotto o-negai shimasu!*
Wait for me! *Matte kudasai!*
waiting: I'm sorry to have kept you w. *O-machi-dō-sama deshita.*
waiting room *machiai-shi-tsu*
waitress *uētoresu*
Wake up! *Okinasai!*
walk: I'm going for a w. *Sampo shite kimasu.*
wall *kabe*

stone w. *ishi-bei*
wallet *saifu*
wallpaper *kabe-gami*
walnut *kurumi*
want: Do you w. any? *Irimasen ka?*
Do you w. this? *Kore, iri-masen ka?*
I don't w. any. *Nani mo irimasen.*
I w. some, please. *Sukoshi kudasai.*
What do you w.? *Nani ga hoshii desu ka?*
want to borrow: I w. t. b. your Bach records. *Ana-ta no Bahha no rekōdo o haishaku shitai desu.*
want to buy: I w. t. b. clothespins. *Sentaku-ba-sami o kaitai desu.*
want to do: I w. t. d. it again. *Mō ichido yaritai desu.*

I w. t. d. it quickly. *Sore o hayaku yaritai desu.*

want to drink: She w. t. d. brandy. *Kanojo wa burandē o nomitai desu.*

want to eat: Do you w. t. e. Japanese food? *Washoku o tabetai desu ka?*

want to get up: I w. t. g. u. at 6 a.m. *Asa no roku-ji ni okitai desu.*

want to go and see: I w. t. g. a. s. a movie. *Eiga o mi ni ikitai desu.*

want to go to: I w. t. g. t. the Ginza. *Ginza e ikitai desu.*

want to make: I w. t. m. a dress. *Doresu o tsukuritai desu.*

want to ride in (on): I w. t. r. o. the monorail. *Monorēru ni notte ikitai desu.*

want to see: Do you w. t. s. this magazine? *Kono zasshi o mitai desu ka?*

want to sell: Does he w. t. s. that refrigerator? *Sono reizōko o uritai desu ka?*

want to sleep: Do you w. t.

s.? *Nemutai desu ka?*

want to sleep late: I w. t. s. l. *Osoku made netai desu.*

want to talk to: I w. t. t. t. the manager. *Manējā ni hanashitai desu.*

want to try on: I w. t. t. o. this dress. *Kono doresu o kite mitai desu.*

I w. t. t. o. those shoes. *Sono kutsu o haite mitai desu.*

I w. t. t. o. that hat. *Sono bōshi o kabutte mitai desu.*

want to try out: I w. t. t. o. that motorcycle. *Sono ōtobai ni notte mitai desu.*

want to visit (go see): My husband w. t. v. Kyoto. *Shujin wa Kyōto e ikitai desu.*

war *sensō*

ward office *kuyakusho*

wardrobe (portable clothes closet) *yōfuku-dansu*

warm *atatakai*

Are you w. enough? *Jūbun atatakai desu ka?*

I'm w. enough. *Jūbun ata-*

takai desu.

Is it w.? (to the touch) *Atatakai desu ka?*

Is it w. out? *Soto wa atatakai desu ka?*

It's w. (to the touch) *Atatakai desu.*

It's w. out. *Soto wa atata-kai desu.*

wart *ibo*

wash & wear *nō-airon*

washbasin (sink) *semmendai*

washboard *sentaku-ita*

washcloth *tenugui*

washer (electric, clothes) *sentakuki*

washing (laundry) *sentaku-mono*

washing machine *sentaku-ki*

washtub *tarai*

washwoman *sentaku-onna*

waste: Don't w. it. *Muda ni shinai yō ni.*

Don't w. your time. *Jikan o muda ni shinai yō ni.*

wastebasket *kuzukago*

wasting: I'm w. my time. *Watashi wa jikan o mu-da ni shite imasu.*

You're w. your time.

Anata wa jikan o muda ni shite imasu.

watch (timepiece) *tokei*

watchman *bannin*

Watch out! *Abunai!*

watch repairman *tokei-shūrikō*

Watch your step! *Ashimoto ni ki o tsukete kudasai!*

water *o-mizu*

a glass of w. *mizu ippai*

cold w. *tsumetai mizu*

drinking w. *nomi-mizu*

fresh w. *shinsen na mizu*

hot w. *o-yu*

hot w. (for drinking) *sayu*

ice w. *aisu-uōtā*

lukewarm w. *nurumayu*

mineral w. *tansansui*

rain w. *ama-mizu*

salt w. *shio-mizu*

Turn off the w., please. *Suidō o shimete kudasai.*

Turn on the w., please. *Suidō o akete kudasai.*

watercolor (painting) *sui-saiga*

waterfall *taki*

water faucet *jaguchi*

water goblet *gurasu*

watering can *jōro*

watermelon *suika*

waterproof *bōsui no*

water pump (car) *uōtā-pompu*

water skiing *suijō-suki*

water skis *uōtā-suki*

water softener *kōsui-chū-wazai*

watery *mizuppoi*

wave *nami*

wax *wakkusu*

  sealing w. *fūrō*

waxer (for floors) *wakkusā*

wax paper *rō-gami*

way: Can you show me the w.? *Annai shite kudasaimasu ka?*

  Get out of the w., please. *Doite kudasai.*

  half w. *chūto*

  I've lost my w. *Michi ni mayotte shimaimashita.*

  out of the w. *hempi na tokoro*

  that w. (in that direction) *achira e*

  that w. (in that manner) *sō*

  this w. (in this direction) *kochira e*

  this w. (in this manner) *kō*

  Which w. is it? *Dochira desu ka?*

W.C. *toire*

we *watashitachi wa (ga)*

weak *yowai*

wealthy *kanemochi no*

wear well: Will these trousers w. w.? *Kono zubon wa yoku mochimasu ka?*

weather *o-tenki*

  Is the w. bad out? *O-tenki ga warui desu ka?*

  Is the w. good out? *O-tenki ga ii desu ka?*

  The w. is bad. *Warui o-tenki desu.*

  The w. is clearing. *Harete kimashita.*

  The w. is good. *Ii o-tenki desu.*

weather forecast *tenki-yohō*

weather stripping *sukima tēpu*

wedding *kekkonshiki*

wedding anniversary *kekkon-kinembi*

wedding cake *uedingu-kēki*

wedding ring *kekkon-yubi-wa*

Wednesday *Suiyōbi*

weed *zassō*

week: all w. *isshūkan*
a w. ago *isshūkan mae*
every w. *maishū*
last w. *senshū*
next w. *raishū*
once a w. *isshūkan ni ichido*
one w. from today *kyō kara isshūkan-go*
this w. *konshū*
twice a w. *isshūkan ni nido*

weekday *heijitsu*

weekend *shūmatsu*

weekly *maishū*

weekly magazine *shūkanshi*

weigh: How much does this w.? *Kono mekata wa dono gurai deshō ka?*
How much do you w.? *Anata wa nankiro taijū ga arimasu ka?*
I w. ... kilos. *Watashi wa ... kiro arimasu.*

weight: Have you gained w.? *Futorimashita ka?*
Have you lost w.? *Yasemashita ka?*
I've gained w. *Futorimashita.*
I've lost w. *Yasemashita.*

You've gained w. *Anata wa futorimashita, ne.*
You've lost w. *Anata wa yasemashita, ne.*

Welcome! *Yoku irasshaimashita!*

welcome: You're w. (response to Thank you) *Dō itashimashite.*

Well. (surprise) (masc.) *Oya.* (fem.) *Mā.*

well-behaved *gyōgi no ii*

well-done: (of broiled steak) Make mine w.-d., please. *Yoku yaite kudasai.*

Well done! *Umai desu!*

well-dressed *o-share no*

well-groomed *minari no ii*

west *nishi*

wet *nureta*

wet suit *uetto-sūtsu*

wharf *hatoba*

What? (interrogative) *Nan desu ka?*

What! (exclamatory) *Nani!*

What am I going to do? *Dō shimashō?*

What are you doing? *Nani o shite imasu ka?*

What are you going to do? *Dō shimasu ka?*

What did he (she) say? *Nan to iimashita ka?*

What did you say? *Nan to osshaimashita ka?*

What does this mean? *Kore wa dō yū imi desu ka?*

What do you mean? *Dō yū imi desu ka?*

What do you think (about it)? *Dō omoimasu ka?*

What do you want? *Nani ga hoshii desu ka?*

What happened? *Dō shimashita ka?*

What is it? *Nan desu ka?*

What kind is it? *Donna no desu ka?*

What size is it? *Kono saizu wa ikutsu desu ka?*

What's the exchange rate? *Kawase-sōba wa ikura desu ka?*

What's the matter? *Dō shimashita ka?*

What's the temperature out? *Soto no ondo wa nando desu ka?*

What's the trouble? *Dō shimashita ka?*

What's the use? *Shikata ga nai.*

What's this (that)? *Kore (sore) wa nan desu ka?*

What's this called in Japanese? *Kore wa Nihongo de nan to iimasu ka?*

What's wrong? *Dō shimashita ka?*

What's your name? *Nan to osshaimasu ka?*

What time are you arriving? *Nanji ni tsukimasu ka?*

What time are you leaving? *Nanji ni tachimasu ka?*

What time does it arrive? *Nanji ni tsukimasu ka?*

What time does it close? *Nanji ni shimemasu ka?*

What time does it leave? *Nanji ni demasu ka?*

What time does it open? *Nanji ni akimasu ka?*

What time is it? *Nanji desu ka?*

wheat *komugi*

wheel *wa*
    steering w. *handoru*

wheelchair *kuruma-isu*

When? *Itsu?*

When are you going? *Itsu ikimasu ka?*

When did it happen? *Itsu okorimashita ka?*

When did you arrive? *Itsu tsukimashita ka?*

When does it (the train) start? *Nanji ni demasu ka?*

When does it (the play) start? *Nanji ni hajimarimasu ka?*

When is your birthday? *Anata no tanjōbi wa itsu desu ka?*

When will it be ready? *Itsu dekimasu ka?*

When will you be back? *Itsu kaerimasu ka?*

When will you be ready? *Itsu jumbi ga dekimasu ka?*

Where? *Doko?*

Where can I buy ...? *... wa doko de kaemasu ka?*

Where can I find a telephone? *Denwa wa doko ni arimasu ka?*

Where can I send a telegram? *Dempō wa doko de dasemasu ka?*

Where do you come from? *O-kuni wa dochira desu ka?*

Where do you live? *Doko ni sunde irasshaimasu ka?*

Where is ...? *... wa doko desu ka?*

Where is it? *Doko desu ka?*

Where's a gas station? I've run out of gas. *Sutando wa doko desu ka? Gasorin ga kiremashita.*

Where's the information desk? *Annaijo wa doko desu ka?*

Where's the ladies' room? *Keshōshitsu wa doko desu ka?*

Where's the men's room? *O-toire wa doko desu ka?*

Where were you born? *Anata wa doko de umaremashita ka?*

Which one? (of two) *Dochira?*

Which one? (of more than two) *Dore?*

Which one is better? *Dotchi ga ii desu ka?*

Which track does the

train leave from? *Kisha wa nambansen kara demasu ka?*

Which way is it? *Dono hōmen desu ka?*

whipped cream *hoippu-kurīmu*

whisk broom *yōfuku-burashi*

whiskey *uisukī*
  bourbon w. *bābon*
  double w. *daburu uisukī*
  Scotch w. *Sukotchi*

whiskey & soda *uisukī-sōda*

whiskey & water *mizuwari*

whiskey sour *uisukī-sawā*

whisper: W.! *Mimi-uchi shite kudasai!*

whistle: Can you w.? *Kuchibue ga fukemasu ka?*

white *shiroi*

white bread *shiro-pan*

white cake *howaito-kēki*

white-collar worker *sararī-man*

white gold *hakkin*

white hair *shiraga*

white shirt *waishatsu*

white sidewalls (tires) *shiro-taiya*

white wine *shiro-budōshu*

Who? *Donata?*

Who are you? *Donata desu ka?*

Who did this? *Dare ga kore o shimashita ka?*

Who is he (she)? *Ano hito wa dare desu ka?*

Who is it? *Donata desu ka?*

Who's there? *Soko ni iru no wa donata desu ka?*

whole *zentai*

wholesale *oroshi-uri*

wholesaler *oroshiya*

whole-wheat bread *kuro-pan*

Whose? *Donata no?*

Whose is this? *Kore wa donata no desu ka?*

Why? *Dō shite?*

wide *hiroi*

widow *mibōjin*

widower *otoko-yamome*

wife (his, your) *okusan*, (my) *kanai*

wig *katsura*

wild boar *inoshishi*

wildflower *no-no-hana*

will (testament) *yuigon-jō*

willing: Are you w. to do it? *Yaru ki ga arimasu ka?*

Are you w. to go? *O-ide ni natte mo ii desu ka?*

I'm w. to do it. *Yaru ki ga arimasu.*

I'm w. to go. *Itte mo ii desu.*

Will you have a cigarette? *Tabako o meshiagarimasu ka?*

Will you have some? *Sukoshi ikaga desu ka?*

Will you have some more? *Mō sukoshi ikaga desu ka?*

wind *kaze*

wind: Don't forget to w. your watch. *Wasurezu ni tokei o maite oite kudasai.*

I forgot to w. my watch. *Tokei o maku no o wasuremashita.*

window *mado*

Close the w., please. *Mado o shimete kudasai.*

Open the w., please. *Mado o akete kudasai.*

store w. *shō-uindō*

storm w. *nijū-mado*

ticket w. *mado-guchi*

window curtain *kāten*

window shutter *shattā*

windowsill *mado-jiki-i*

windshield *furonto-garasu*

windshield wiper *waipā*

windy: Is it w. out? *Kaze ga fuite imasu ka?*

It's w. out. *Kaze ga fuite imasu.*

wine: *budōshu*

a bottle of w. *budōshu ippon*

red w. *reddo-wain*

sparkling w. *awadachi-wain*

white w. *shiro-budōshu*

wine glass *wain-gurasu*

wine list *wain-risuto*

wing *tsubasa*

winter *fuyu*

wintertime *fuyu*

Wipe this, please. *Yoku kore o fuite kudasai.*

wire (metal) *harigane*

wisdom tooth *oyashirazu*

wisteria *fuji*

with ... *to tomo ni*

withered *kareta*

without ... *nashi ni*

woman *onna no hito*

wonder: I w. why. *Dō shite deshō.*

I w. why not. *Dō shite sō de wa nai deshō.*

wonderful *subarashii*

That's w.! *Sore wa suba-rashii desu!*

wood *mokuzai*

firew. *maki*

kindling w. *takigi*

woodblock print *hanga*

wooden *ki no*

wooden clogs *geta*

woods *mori*

woodwork *mokuseihin*

wool (material) *yōmō*

wool (yarn) *ke-ito*

work: Does it w.? *Kore wa kikimasu ka?*

It doesn't w. *Kikimasen.*

work: What kind of w. do you do? *Go-shokugyō wa nan desu ka?*

working day *heijitsu*

workshop *kōba*

world *sekai*

worn: I'm w. out. *Kutakuta desu.*

It's w. out. *Mō tsukai-mono ni narimasen.*

worried: Aren't you w.? *Shimpai de wa arimasen ka?*

Are you w.? *Shimpai desu ka?*

I'm w. *Shimpai desu.*

I'm not w. *Shimpai de wa arimasen.*

worry: Don't w.! *Shimpai shinai de kudasai!*

worse *motto warui*

Is it w.? *Waruku narima-shita ka?*

It's w. *Waruku narima-shita.*

worthless *neuchi no nai*

Wrap it up, please. *Tsu-tsunde kudasai.*

wrapping paper *tsutsumi-gami*

wrench: monkey w. *monkī-supanā*

socket w. *soketto-renchi*

wringer (on washing machine) *shiboriki*

wrinkle (material or skin) *shiwa*

wrinkled (material or skin) *shiwa no yotta*

wrist *tekubi*

wristwatch *ude-dokei*

Write it down, please. *So-re o kaite kudasai.*

Write this in *kanji*, please.

Kore o Nihon no ji de
kaite kudasai.

writing pad memo

writing paper binsen

wrong: I'm w. Watashi ga
machigatte imasu.

Something's w. Nani ka
arimashita, ne.

That's w. Sore wa chigai-
masu.

What's w.? Dō shimashita
ka?

You're w. Anata wa ma-
chigatte imasen ka?

wrong number (telephone)
bangō-chigai

You have the w. n. Bangō
ga machigatte imasu.

X

Xerox Zerokkusu

X-ray rentogen

Y

yacht (sailboat) yotto

yard (garden) nakaniwa

yarn (for knitting) ke-ito

a ball of y. ke-ito hitomaki

yawn (a) akubi

year toshi

all y. ichinenjū

a y. ago ichinen mae

every y. mainen

last y. kyonen

leap y. urū-doshi

next y. rainen

once a y. ichinen ni ichido

the y. before last ototoshi

this y. kotoshi

twice a y. ichinen ni nido

yearly mainen no

yeast īsuto

yellow *kiiroi*
yellow gold *kin*
Yes. *Hai.*
yesterday *kinō*
  day before y. *ototoi*
yesterday afternoon *kinō no gogo*
yesterday evening *kinō no yūgata*
yesterday morning *kinō no asa*
yesterday noon *kinō no hiru*
yet: not y. *mada*
yolk *kimi*
you (subject, singular) *anata wa (ga)*
  (subject, plural) *anatagata wa (ga)*
  (object, singular) *anata o*
  (object, plural) *anatagata o*

for (to) y. (singular) *anata ni*
for (to) y. (plural) *anatagata ni*
young *wakai*
young lady (unmarried) *o-jō-san*
young man (unmarried) *seinen*
your (singular) *anata no*
  (plural) *anatagata no*
yours: Is it y.? *Anata no desu ka?*
  It's not y. *Anata no de wa arimasen.*
  It's y. *Anata no desu.*
yourself: Can you do it y.? *Anata ni dekimasu ka?*
  You can do it y. *Anata ni dekimasu.*
youthful *wakawakashii*

Z

zero *zero*
zigzag *jiguzagu*
zip code *yūbin-bangō*
zipper *jippā*

zodiac: the signs of the z. (J.) *jūnishi*, (W.) *jūnikyū*
zone: safety z. *anzen-chitai*
zoo *dōbutsu-en*

APPENDICES

PHRASES FOR EVERYDAY SITUATIONS

Salutations and Civilities

Good morning! (till about 10 a.m.)	*O-hayō gozaimasu!*
Good afternoon (*or* Hello)!	*Konnichi wa!*
Good evening! (after dark)	*Komban wa!*
It's been a long time since I last met you, hasn't it?	*Shibaraku desu ne?*
How do you do? (at first meeting)	*Hajimemashite.*
How are you?	*Ikaga desu ka?*
I'm very happy to meet you.	*Dōzo yoroshiku.*
I'm fine, thank you, and you?	*Arigatō gozaimasu. ...-san wa ikaga desu ka?*
May I introduce you to Mr. ...?	*...-san o go-shōkai itashimasu.*
I'm very happy to meet you.	*Dōzo yoroshiku.*
It was nice meeting you.	*O-me ni kakarete ureshū go-zaimasu.*
Goodbye!	*Sayōnara!*
Good night!	*O-yasumi nasai!*
Sorry to disturb you. (on entering someone's house)	*O-jama shimasu.*
Hello! Anyone there? (on the telephone or in a seemingly unoccupied room or shop)	*Moshi, moshi!*

Please wait a minute.	*Chotto matte kudasai.*
Please excuse me, but...	*Shitsurei shimasu ga...*
I'm home!	*Tadaima!*
Welcome home! (to returning members of the household)	*O-kaeri nasai!*
Pardon me.	*Gomen nasai.*
Yes, I'll have some.	*Itadakimasu.*
Thanks for your hospitality.	*Go-chisō-sama deshita.*
Please come again.	*Mata dōzo.*
Will you help me, please? (in a shop, office, etc.)	*O-negai shimasu!*
Thank you for many favors.	*Iro-iro to dōmo.*
I'm going out now!	*Itte kimasu!*
Goodbye for now! (said by person staying).	*Itte irasshai!*
Congratulations!	*O-medetō gozaimasu!*

Instructions to a Taxi Driver

Do you know where this address is?	*Kono jūsho ga wakarimasu ka?*
I know. I'll show you how to go.	*Wakatte imasu kara, annai shimasu.*
Go straight ahead.	*Massugu itte kudasai.*
Turn right (left).	*Migi (hidari) e magatte kudasai.*
Turn here.	*Koko o magatte kudasai.*
Drive more slowly, please.	*Motto yukkuri hashitte kudasai.*

Go a little farther.	*Mō sukoshi saki e itte kudasai.*
Stop here.	*Koko de ii desu.*
Stop over there.	*Asoko de tomatte kudasai.*
Turn right (left) at the traffic light.	*Kōtsū-shingō de migi (hidari) e magatte kudasai.*
Wait here, please.	*Koko de matte kudasai.*

General Shopping Phrases

I'm going shopping.	*Kaimono ni itte kimasu.*
Where's a department store?	*Depāto wa doko desu ka.*
Can you help me, please?	*Chotto o-negai shimasu.*
I would like to see a	*... ga mitai no desu ga.*
I would like to see that one.	*Are o misete kudasai.*
Will you show me that, please?	*Are o misete kudasai.*
I like this (that) one.	*Kore (sore) ga suki desu.*
I don't like that (this) one.	*Sore (kore) wa kirai desu.*
How much is this?	*Kore wa ikura desu ka?*
I would like to see a larger (smaller) one.	*Motto ōkii (chiisai) no o misete kudasai.*
I would like to buy two of these.	*Kore o futatsu itadakimasu.*
What is this called in Japanese?	*Nihongo de nan to iimasu ka?*
How much is it altogether?	*Zembu de ikura desu ka?*
It's too expensive.	*Chotto takai desu.*
I'll take this one.	*Kore o kudasai.*
When will it be ready?	*Itsu dekiagarimasu ka?*

Will you deliver it?	*Haitatsu shite kudasaimasu ka?*
My address is	*Watashi no jūsho wa ... desu.*
Please deliver to this address.	*Koko e todokete kudasai.*
I'll pay you now.	*Ima haraimasu.*
Send me a bill.	*Seikyūshō o okutte kudasai.*
I'll pay when it is delivered.	*Haitatsu shita toki haraimasu.*

At the Beauty Shop

I want a shampoo-set.	*Shampū-setto o shite kudasai.*
I want a permanent.	*Pāma o kakete kudasai.*
I want a manicure.	*Manikyua o shite kudasai.*
I want a haircut.	*Katto shite kudasai.*
Use cream rinse.	*Kurīmu rinsu o shite kudasai.*
I want my hair bleached.	*Kami o burīchi shite kudasai.*
I want a color rinse.	*Karā rinsu o shite kudasai.*
I want my hair dyed.	*Kami o somete kudasai.*
I want my hair streaked.	*Kami no ke o shima ni somete kudasai.*
I want an oil treatment.	*Oiru shampū o shite kudasai.*
I want a facial.	*Kao no massāji o shite kudasai.*
Cut my hair shorter, please.	*Kami no ke o motto mijikaku shite kudasai.*
Back comb my hair, please.	*Sakage o tatete kudasai.*

At the Barbershop

I want a haircut.	*Sampatsu o shite kudasai.*
I want a light trim.	*Nagame ni shite kudasai.*
I want a shave.	*Hige o sotte kudasai.*
Use scissors on the sides.	*Yoko wa hasami o tsukatte kudasai.*
Don't cut it too short.	*Ammari mijikaku shinai de kudasai.*
Cut more off the sides (top).	*Yoko (teppen) o motto katte kudasai.*
I want a shampoo.	*Shampū o shite kudasai.*
I want a face massage.	*Kao o massāji shite kudasai.*
Don't use hair spray, please.	*Heā-supurē o kakenai de kudasai.*
Don't use the curling iron, please.	*Airon o tsukawanai de kudasai.*

At the Dressmaker or Tailor Shop

I want to have a dress (suit) made.	*Yōfuku (sebiro) o koshiraete moraitai desu.*
I like this style.	*Kono kata ga suki desu.*
How much material does it take?	*Dono gurai kiji ga irimasu ka?*
How much will you charge?	*Ikura desu ka?*
Take my measurements, please.	*Sumpō o totte kudasai.*
When shall I come for a fitting?	*Itsu karinui ga dekimasu ka?*

It fits very well.	*Chōdo ii desu.*
Let it out here.	*Koko o yuruku shite kudasai.*
It's too loose (tight) here.	*Koko ga yurui (kitsui) desu.*
Take it in here.	*Koko o tsumete kudasai.*
It's too short (long).	*Mijika-sugimasu (naga-sugimasu).*
When will it be finished?	*Itsu dekiagarimasu ka?*
How much is one meter of this cloth?	*Kono kiji wa ichi mētoru ikura desu ka?*
May I see some cloth samples?	*Kiji no mihon o misete kudasai.*
Is this wool (cotton, silk, nylon)?	*Kore wa jummō (momen, kinu, nairon) desu ka?*

At the Service Station

Change the flat tire.	*Taiya o kaete kudasai.*
Change the oil.	*Oiru o kaete kudasai.*
Charge the battery.	*Batterī o jūden shite kudasai.*
Check the battery, oil, and water.	*Batterī to oiru to mizu o mite kudasai.*
Check the tires (for air).	*Kūki-atsu o mite kudasai.*
Fill it up (with gas).	*Mantan ni shite kudasai.*
Fix the	*... o naoshite kudasai.*
Flush the radiator.	*Rajiētā no mizu o kaete kudasai.*
Give me ... liters of gas.	*Gasorin o ... rittoru irete kudasai.*
I want an engine tune-up.	*Enjin no chunnappu o shite kudasai.*

Lubricate the car.	*Gurīsu-appu shite kudasai.*
Rotate the tires.	*Taiya no ichi o kōkan shite kudasai.*
The tires take 1.50 kgs. pressure. (small car tires)	*Itten-go irete kudasai.*
Wipe off the windshield.	*Furonto-garasu o fuite kudasai.*

AUTO PARTS AND ACCESSORIES

accelerator	*akuseru*
automatic transmission	*ōtomachikku toransumisshon*
backup light	*bakku-rampu*
battery	*batterī*
body	*bodē*
brake	*burēki*
foot b.	*futto-burēki*
hand b.	*hando-burēki*
brake rod	*burēki-roddo*
bumper	*bampā*
carburetor	*kyaburētā*
chains	*chēn*
clutch	*kuratchi*
clutch pedal	*kuratchi-pedaru*
dashboard	*dasshubōdo*
dimmer switch	*dimā-suitchi*
distributor	*disutoribyūtā*
door	*doa*
door handle	*doa-handoru*
engine	*enjin*
engine block	*enjin-burokku*

exhaust pipe	*haikikan*
fan	*fan*
fan belt	*fan-beruto*
fender	*fendā*
gas tank	*gasorin-tanku*
gear	*giyā*
generator	*jenerētā*
headlight	*heddoraito*
heater	*hītā*
hood	*bonnetto*
horn	*kurakushon*
hub cap	*habu-kyappu*
ignition	*sutātā-suitchi*
inner tube	*chūbu*
jack	*jakki*
knob	*totte*
light switch	*denki no suitchi*
motor	*mōtā*
muffler	*mafurā*
oil filter	*oiru-fuirutā*
piston	*pisuton*
points	*pointo*
radiator	*rajiētā*
rearview mirror	*bakku-mirā*
roof	*yane*
spare tire	*supeā-taiya*
spark plug	*supāku-puragu*
starter	*sutātā*
steering wheel	*handoru*
taillight	*tēru-rampu*
tailpipe	*haikikan*

tire	*taiya*
flat t.	*panku*
tire pump	*kūki-ire*
tool kit	*dōgu-bako*
trunk	*toranku*
trunk lid	*toranku no futa*
tube	*chūbu*
tubeless tire	*chūburesu-taiya*
turn signal	*hōkō-shijiki*
valve	*barubu*
vent	*tsūfūkō*
water pump	*uōtā-pompu*
wheel	*hoīru*
white sidewalls	*shiro-taiya*
window	*mado*
windshield	*furonto-garasu*
windshield wiper	*waipā*

TIRE PRESSURE

lbs. per sq. in.		kgs. per sq. cm. (approx.)
20		1.40 *itten-yon*
22	(avg. small cars)	1.50 *itten-go*
24		1.70 *itten-nana*
26		1.80 *itten-hachi*
28	(avg. large cars)	2.00 *niten-rei*
30		2.10 *niten-ichi*

Telephoning

Hello.	*Moshi, moshi.*
Hello, operator?	*Moshi, moshi. Kōkandai desu ka?*
Does anyone there speak English?	*Donata ka Eigo no wakaru kata wa irasshaimasen ka?*
Do you speak English?	*Eigo o hanashimasu ka?*
He (she) is not here.	*Ima orimasen.*
Just a moment, please.	*Shōshō o-machi kudasai.*
May I speak to Mr. ...?	*...-san ni o-hanashi shitai no desu ga.*
Who's speaking?	*Donata desu ka?*
Who do you wish to speak to?	*Donata ni o-kake desu ka?*
You have the wrong number.	*Bangō ga chigaimasu.*
Goodbye.	*Sayōnara.*
Please call me tomorrow.	*Ashita renraku shite kudasai.*
This is	*Watashi wa ... to mōshimasu ga.*
Please call Mr. (Mrs., Miss) ... to the telephone.	*...-san o denwa ni yonde kudasai.*
Please tell him to call me.	*Kare ni denwa o watashi ni kudasaru yō ni tsutaete kudasai.*

Health Problems

I'm bleeding.	*Chi ga dete imasu.*
I burned myself.	*Yakedo shimashita.*
I don't feel good.	*Kibun ga warui desu.*

I feel dizzy.	*Me ga mawarimasu.*
I feel faint.	*Ki ga tōku narisō desu.*
I feel fine.	*Genki desu.*
I feel nauseated.	*Hakike ga shimasu.*
I have a cold.	*Kaze o hikimashita.*
I have a cough.	*Seki ga demasu.*
I have a fever.	*Netsu ga arimasu.*
I have a headache.	*Atama ga itai desu.*
I have an earache.	*Mimi ga itai desu.*
I have a nosebleed.	*Hanaji ga demasu.*
I have a pain here.	*Koko ga itai desu.*
I have a sore throat.	*Nodo ga itai desu.*
I have a sprained ankle.	*Ashikubi o nenza shimashita.*
I have a stiff neck.	*Kubi o nechigaemashita.*
I have a stomach ache.	*O-naka ga itai desu.*
I have a toothache.	*Ha ga itai desu.*
I have chills.	*Samuke ga shimasu.*
I've cut myself here.	*Koko o kitte shimaimashita.*
I have indigestion.	*O-naka o kowashimashita.*
I have the hiccups.	*Shakkuri ga demasu.*
I have a hangover.	*Futsuka-yoi desu.*
I vomited.	*Hakimashita.*
Please call a doctor.	*O-isha-san o yonde kudasai.*
Please take me to a doctor.	*Watashi o o-isha ni tsurete itte kudasai.*
My blood type is A (B, AB, O).	*Watashi no ketsueki-gata wa ē (bī, ēbī, ō) desu.*

Interviewing a Maid

Hello. (daytime)	*Konnichi wa.*
Come in, please.	*Dōzo o-hairi kudasai.*
Sit down, please.	*Dōzo o-kake kudasai.*
What is your name?	*O-namae wa nan to osshaimasu ka?*
Where do you live?	*Doko ni sunde irasshaimasu ka?*
Are you married?	*Kekkon shite imasu ka?*
How many children do you have?	*O-kosan wa nannin irasshaimasu ka?*
How old are you?	*O-ikutsu desu ka?*
I need someone for general housework.	*Kaseifu-san ga hoshii no desu ga.*
Will you take care of children?	*Kodomo no sewa o shite kudasaimasu ka?*
Can you cook Western food?	*Anata wa seiyō-ryōri ga tsukuremasu ka?*
Will you live in?	*Sumi-komi de yoroshii desu ka?*
I would like you to work five (six, seven) days a week.	*Shū itsuka (muika, nanoka) hataraite kudasaimasu ka?*
The salary is ... yen a month.	*Gekkyū wa ...-en desu.*
I will give you ... months' pay as bonus at New Years.	*Bōnasu wa ... kagetsu-bun o-shōgatsu ni haraimasu.*
I will give you ... weeks' paid vacation.	*...-shūkan yūkyū-kyūka ga arimasu.*
When can you start work?	*Itsu kara kite itadakemasu ka?*

Good! Then it's agreed.	*Dōmo arigatō gozaimasu. De wa sō itashimashō.*
Goodbye!	*Sayōnara!*

Housekeeping Instructions

Answer the doorbell.	*Genkan ni dete kudasai.*
Answer the telephone.	*Denwa ni dete kudasai.*
Can you stay late tonight?	*Kon·ya osoku made ite kudasaimasu ka?*
Change the sheets and pillowcases.	*Shītsu to makura-kabā o kaete kudasai.*
Clean the silver.	*Ginshokki o migaite kudasai.*
Clean the stove.	*Renji o kirei ni shite kudasai.*
Clean the toilet.	*O-te-arai o kirei ni shite kudasai.*
Clear the table.	*Sagete kudasai.*
Defrost and clean the refrigerator.	*Reizōko no shimo o totte, kirei ni shite kudasai.*
Dust the furniture.	*Kagu o hataite kudasai.*
Empty the ashtray.	*Haizara o akete kudasai.*
Empty the garbage.	*Gomi o sutete kudasai.*
Empty the wastebasket.	*Kuzukago o akete kudasai.*
Guests are coming this evening.	*O-kyaku-sama ga kon·ya kimasu.*
Hang up the clothes.	*Yōfuku o kakete kudasai.*
Iron this (these).	*Kore ni airon o kakete kudasai.*
I'm going out.	*Itte kimasu.*
I'll be back shortly.	*Sugu kaerimasu.*

Leave the light on (off).	*Denki o tsukeppanashi ni shite kudasai. (Denki o keshite oite kudasai.)*
Leave the door open (closed).	*Doa o akete (shimete) oite kudasai.*
Leave the window open (closed).	*Mado o akete (shimete) oite kudasai.*
Light the fire.	*Hi o tsukete kudasai.*
Lock the door.	*Doa ni kagi o kakete kudasai.*
Make the beds.	*Beddo o naoshite kudasai.*
Mop the floors.	*Yuka o fuite kudasai.*
Preheat the oven.	*Ōbun o atatamete oite kudasai.*
Scour the pots and pans.	*O-nabe to furaipan o migaite kudasai.*
Scour the tub and sink.	*Yokusō to semmendai o kirei ni shite kudasai.*
Send this to the cleaners.	*Kore o dorai-kuriningu ni dashite kudasai.*
Set the table.	*Tēburu o tsukutte kudasai.*
Starch this.	*Kore ni nori o tsukete kudasai.*
Straighten the furniture.	*Kagu o kichin to shite kudasai.*
Sweep the floor.	*Yuka o haite kudasai.*
Throw this away.	*Kore o sutete kudasai.*
Turn the mattress.	*Matto o uragaeshite kudasai.*
Turn on (off) the lights.	*Denki o tsukete (keshite) kudasai.*
Use furniture polish.	*Kagu-migaki o tsukatte kudasai.*
Vacuum the rugs.	*Jūtan ni denki-sōjiki o kakete kudasai.*

Wash the windows (mirrors).	*Mado-garasu (kagami) o a-ratte kudasai.*
Wash the dishes.	*O-sara o aratte kudasai.*
Wash this (these) in the machine.	*Kore o sentakuki de aratte kudasai.*
Wash this (these) by hand.	*Kore o te de aratte kudasai.*
Water the plants (flowers).	*Hachi-ue ni mizu o yatte kudasai.*
Wax the floors.	*Yuka o wakkusu de migaite kudasai.*

Instructions for Child Care

Change his diapers.	*O-mutsu o torikaete kudasai.*
Comb his hair.	*Kami o kushi de toite kudasai.*
Feed him his lunch (breakfast, supper).	*O-hirugohan (asagohan, bangohan) o tabesasete kudasai.*
Give him a bath.	*O-furo ni irete kudasai.*
Give him a bottle.	*Miruku o agete kudasai.*
Push him in the stroller.	*Ubaguruma ni nosete tsurete itte kudasai.*
Put him to bed at ... o'clock.	*...-ji ni nekasete kudasai.*
Take him for a walk.	*O-sampo ni tsurete itte kudasai.*
Take him to the playground.	*Yūenchi ni tsurete itte kudasai.*
Wash his hands and face.	*Kao to te o aratte yatte kudasai.*

At the Train (Subway) Station

One (ticket) for ..., please.	*... ichimai kudasai.*
Two adult's (tickets).	*Otona nimai.*
Three children's (tickets).	*Kodomo sammai.*
How much is it?	*Ikura desu ka?*
Does it stop at (in) ...?	*... ni tomarimasu ka?*
First class.	*Ittō.*
Second class.	*Nitō.*
Express ticket (special-express ticket), please.	*Kyūkōken (tōkkyūken) o kudasai.*
Reserved-seat ticket, please.	*Zaseki shiteiken o kudasai.*

At the Theater

What time does it start?	*Nanji ni hajimarimasu ka?*
What time does it end?	*Nanji ni owarimasu ka?*
There are no more seats.	*Man·in desu.*
Are there any reserved seats?	*Shitei-seki ga arimasu ka?*
I want to make a reservation for	*... no yoyaku o shitai ,no desu ga.*

At the Hotel

I'd like a room.	*Heya ga aite imasu ka?*
Western-style room.	*Yōma.*
Japanese-style room.	*Nihomma.*
Are you alone?	*O-hitori desu ka?*
There are two of us.	*Futari desu.*

With bath, please.	*Basutsuki ni shite kudasai.*
I'd like to pay the bill.	*O-kanjō o o-negai shimasu.*

Renting a Room (Apartment/House)

I want to rent a room (apartment/house).	*Heya (apāto/ie) o karitai no desu ga.*
For one week (one month).	*Isshūkan (ikkagetsukan).*
For one year.	*Ichinenkan.*
I'd like it furnished.	*Kagutsuki ga ii no desu ga.*
How many rooms are there?	*Ikutsu heya ga arimasu ka?*
How much is the room (house) rent?	*Heyadai (yachin) wa ikura desu ka?*
Is deposit money needed?	*Shikikin ga hitsuyō desu ka?*
May I pay by check?	*Kogitte de ii desu ka?*

At the Post Office

One (two) ¥15 stamp, please.	*Jūgo-en kitte o ichimai (nimai) kudasai.*
Special delivery, please.	*Sokutatsu ni shite kudasai.*
Register this, please.	*Kakitome ni shite kudasai.*
By airmail, please.	*Kōkūbin de, o-negai shimasu.*
By seamail, please.	*Funabin de, o-negai shimasu.*
I want to insure it.	*Hoken o kaketai no desu ga.*
I want a money order, please.	*Yūbin-kawase o kudasai.*
Send it as a regular parcel, please.	*Futsū kozutsumi ni shite kudasai.*

NUMBERS AND COUNTING

The Numerals and Numeratives

Because of a system of numeratives (also called classifiers or counters), counting in Japanese is an extremely complex problem. These numeratives correspond somewhat to the English slice, pair, head, etc., as in "a slice of bread," "a pair of shoes," "two heads of lettuce," but the Japanese system extends far beyond that of the English. Since a detailed explanation of numeratives is inappropriate in a book of this scope, the explanation is limited to the numerals and several of the most common numeratives.

CHINESE-DERIVED NUMERALS		NATIVE JAPANESE NUMERALS
1	*ichi*	*hitotsu*
2	*ni*	*futatsu*
3	*san*	*mittsu*
4	*shi* (or *yon*)	*yottsu*
5	*go*	*itsutsu*
6	*roku*	*muttsu*
7	*shichi* (or *nana*)	*nanatsu*
8	*hachi*	*yattsu*
9	*ku* (or *kyū*)	*kokonotsu*
10	*jū*	*tō*

Note that the native Japanese numerals extend only to ten, after which the numerals of Chinese derivation must be used. The advantage of the native numerals is that when counting fewer than ten objects they can often be used without numeratives, i.e., *mittsu no tamago* (three eggs), *futatsu no kuruma* (two cars), and *yottsu no taipuraitā* (four typewriters). They cannot be used, however, to count things like people, animals, or money. Explanations are given elsewhere for counting days and months (p. 165), time (p. 167), and money (p. 168). Here is the way to count people, animals and insects, dresses and suits, and footwear.

	People	Animals & Insects	Dresses & Suits	Footwear (in pairs)
1	*hitori*	*ippiki*	*itchaku*	*issoku*
2	*futari*	*nihiki*	*nichaku*	*nisoku*
3	*sannin*	*sambiki*	*sanchaku*	*sanzoku*
4	*yonin*	*yonhiki*	*yonchaku*	*yonsoku*
5	*gonin*	*gohiki*	*gochaku*	*gosoku*
6	*rokunin*	*roppiki*	*rokuchaku*	*rokusoku*
7	*shichinin*	*nanahiki*	*nanachaku*	*nanasoku*
8	*hachinin*	*happiki*	*hatchaku*	*hassoku*
9	*kyūnin*	*kyūhiki*	*kyūchaku*	*kyūsoku*
10	*jūnin*	*jippiki*	*jitchaku*	*jissoku*
11	*jūichinin*	*jūippiki*	*jūitchaku*	*jūissoku*
100	*hyakunin*	*hyappiki*	*hyakuchaku*	*hyakusoku*
How many?	*Nannin?*	*Nambiki?*	*Nanchaku?*	*Nansoku?*

MONTHS OF THE YEAR		COUNTING MONTHS	
Jan.	*Ichi-gatsu*	1 m.	*ikkagetsu*
Feb.	*Ni-gatsu*	2 m.	*nikagetsu*
Mar.	*San-gatsu*	3 m.	*sankagetsu*
Apr.	*Shi-gatsu*	4 m.	*yonkagetsu*
May	*Go-gatsu*	5 m.	*gokagetsu*
June	*Roku-gatsu*	6 m.	*rokkagetsu*
July	*Shichi-gatsu*	7 m.	*shichikagetsu*
Aug.	*Hachi-gatsu*	8 m.	*hakkagetsu*
Sep.	*Ku-gatsu*	9 m.	*kyūkagetsu*
Oct.	*Jū-gatsu*	10 m.	*jikkagetsu*
Nov.	*Jūichi-gatsu*	11 m.	*jūichikagetsu*
Dec.	*Jūni-gatsu*	12 m.	*jūnikagetsu*

COUNTING DAYS

1 d.	*ichinichi*	7 d.	*nanoka*	13 d.	*jūsannichi*
2 d.	*futsuka*	8 d.	*yōka*	14 d.	*jūyokka*
3 d.	*mikka*	9 d.	*kokonoka*	20 d.	*hatsuka*
4 d.	*yokka*	10 d.	*tōka*	24 d.	*nijūyokka*
5 d.	*itsuka*	11 d.	*jūichinichi*	30 d.	*sanjūnichi*
6 d.	*muika*	12 d.	*jūninichi*	40 d.	*yonjūnichi*

The same words for counting days can be used to number the days of the month. For instance, *mikka* means both "three days" and "the third day." Exceptions to this rule are *tsuitachi* (the first) and *misoka* (the last).

ORDINAL NUMBERS

1st	*dai-ichiban*	11th	*dai-jūichiban*
2nd	*dai-niban*	12th	*dai-jūniban*
3rd	*dai-samban*	13th	*dai-jūsamban*
4th	*dai-yomban*	14th	*dai-jūyomban*
5th	*dai-goban*	15th	*dai-jūgoban*
6th	*dai-rokuban*	20th	*dai-nijūban*
7th	*dai-shichiban*	30th	*dai-sanjūban*
8th	*dai-hachiban*	40th	*dai-yonjūban*
9th	*dai-kyūban*	50th	*dai-gojūban*
10th	*dai-jūban*	100th	*dai-hyakuban*

Note that *bamme* can be used in place of *ban*, as in *dai-sambamme no kuruma* (the third car), and the prefix *dai* can be dropped without altering the meaning, i.e., *ichibamme no kōtsū-shingō* (the first traffic light).

Days of the Week

Sunday	*Nichiyōbi*	Friday	*Kin·yōbi*
Monday	*Getsuyōbi*	Saturday	*Doyōbi*
Tuesday	*Kayōbi*	weekday	*heijitsu*
Wednesday	*Suiyōbi*	no-work day	*kyūjitsu*
Thursday	*Mokuyōbi*	weekend	*shūmatsu*

Telling Time

What time is it?	*Nanji desu ka?*
It's one o'clock.	*Ichi-ji desu.*
It's two o'clock.	*Ni-ji desu.*
It's three o'clock.	*San-ji desu.*
It's four o'clock.	*Yo-ji desu.*
It's five o'clock.	*Go-ji desu.*
It's six o'clock.	*Roku-ji desu.*
It's seven o'clock.	*Shichi-ji desu.*
It's eight o'clock.	*Hachi-ji desu.*
It's nine o'clock.	*Ku-ji desu.*
It's ten o'clock.	*Jū-ji desu.*
It's eleven o'clock.	*Jūichi-ji desu.*
It's twelve o'clock.	*Jūni-ji desu.*
It's quarter to one.	*Ichi-ji jūgo-fun mae desu.*
It's quarter past one.	*Ichi-ji jūgo-fun sugi desu.*
It's half past one.	*Ichi-ji han desu.*

1 minute = *ippun*	8 minutes = *hachi-fun*
2 minutes = *ni-fun*	9 minutes = *kyū-fun*
3 minutes = *sampun*	10 minutes = *jippun*
4 minutes = *yompun*	20 minutes = *nijippun*
5 minutes = *go-fun*	30 minutes = *sanjippun*
6 minutes = *roppun*	40 minutes = *yonjippun*
7 minutes = *nana-fun*	50 minutes = *gojippun*

Form other number-minute combinations as follows:

10 *(jū)* +1 min. *(ippun)* = 11 min. *(jū-*
2 *(ni)* × 10 *(jū)* + 2 min. = 22 min. *(nijū.*
3 *(san)* × 10 *(jū)* + 3 min. = 33 min. *(sanjū*

4	(yon)	+ 10 (jū) + 4 min.	= 44 min.	(yonjū-yompun)
5	(go)	+ 10 (jū) + 5 min.	= 55 min.	(gojūgo-fun)

a.m. = *gozen*   p.m. = *gogo*

Money Conversion Tables

DOLLARS TO YEN

$		¥	
1	=	300*	*sambyaku-en*
2	=	600	*roppyaku-en*
3	=	900	*kyūhyaku-en*
4	=	1,200	*sen-nihyaku-en*
5	=	1,500	*sen-gohyaku-en*
6	=	1,800	*sen-happyaku-en*
7	=	2,100	*nisen-hyaku-en*
8	=	2,400	*nisen-yonhyaku-en*
9	=	2,700	*nisen-nanahyaku-en*
10	=	3,000	*sanzen-en*
15	=	4,500	*yonsen-gohyaku-en*
20	=	6,000	*rokusen-en*
25	=	7,500	*nanasen-gohyaku-en*
30	=	9,000	*kyūsen-en*
35	=	10,500	*ichiman-gohyaku-en*
40	=	12,000	*ichiman-nisen-en*
45	=	13,500	*ichiman-sanzen-gohyaku-en*
50	=	15,000	*ichiman-gosen-en*
55	=	16,500	*ichiman-rokusen-gohyaku-en*

* Average rate, September 1976.

60	=	18,000	*ichiman-hassen-en*
65	=	19,500	*ichiman-kyūsen-gohyaku-en*
70	=	21,000	*niman-issen-en*
75	=	22,500	*niman-nisen-gohyaku-en*
80	=	23,000	*niman-sanzen-en*
85	=	24,500	*niman-yonsen-gohyaku-en*
90	=	26,000	*niman-rokusen-en*
95	=	27,000	*niman-nanasen-en*
100	=	30,000	*samman-en*
200	=	60,000	*rokuman-en*
300	=	90,000	*kyūman-en*
400	=	120,000	*jūniman-en*
500	=	150,000	*jūgoman-en*
1,000	=	300,000	*sanjūman-en*

YEN TO DOLLARS

¥		$		¥		$
5	=	.016		100	=	.33
go-en				*hyaku-en*		
10	=	.033		200	=	.66
jū-en				*nihyaku-en*		
20	=	.066		300	=	1.00
nijū-en				*sambyaku-en*		
30	=	.1		400	=	1.33
sanjū-en				*yonhyaku-en*		
40	=	.133		500	=	1.66
yonjū-en				*gohyaku-en*		
50	=	.166		600	=	2.00
gojū-en				*roppyaku-en*		

¥		$	¥		$
700	=	2.33	6,500	=	21.66
nanahyaku-en			*rokusen-gohyaku-en*		
800	=	2.66	7,000	=	23.33
happyaku-en			*nanasen-en*		
900	=	3.00	7,500	=	25.00
kyūhyaku-en			*nanasen-gohyaku-en*		
1,000	=	3.33	8,000	=	26.66
sen-en			*hassen-en*		
1,500	=	5.00	8,500	=	28.33
sen-gohyaku-en			*hassen-gohyaku-en*		
2,000	=	6.66	9,000	=	30.00
nisen-en			*kyūsen-en*		
2,500	=	8.33	9,500	=	31.66
nisen-gohyaku-en			*kyūsen-gohyaku-en*		
3,000	=	10.00	10,000	=	33.33
sanzen-en			*ichiman-en*		
3,500	=	11.66	20,000	=	66.66
sanzen-gohyaku-en			*niman-en*		
4,000	=	13.33	30,000	=	100.00
yonsen-en			*samman-en*		
4,500	=	15.00	40,000	=	133.33
yonsen-gohyaku-en			*yomman-en*		
5,000	=	16.66	50,000	=	166.66
gosen-en			*goman-en*		
5,500	=	18.33	100,000	=	333.33
gosen-gohyaku-en			*jūman-en*		
6,000	=	20.00	1,000,000	=	3,333.33
rokusen-en			*hyakuman-en*		

Tables of Equivalents

LIQUID AND LINEAR MEASURES

ichirittoru (1 liter) = .75 quarts
ichikiro (guramu) (1 kilogram) = 2.2 pounds
issenchi (1 centimeter) = .40 inches
ichimētoru (1 meter) = 1.08 yds or 39 in.
ichikiro (mētoru) (1 kilometer) = .63 miles

1 quart	=	1.2 liters
1 pound	=	.45 kilograms
1 inch	=	2.5 centimeters
1 yard	=	.9 meters
1 mile	=	1.6 kilometers

TEMPERATURE TABLE

FAHREN-HEIT		CENTI-GRADE	FAHREN-HEIT		CENTI-GRADE
0	=	−18	104	=	40
14	=	−10	122	=	50
23	=	−5	212	boiling	100
32	freezing	0	260	=	125
41	=	5	300	=	150
50	=	10	350	=	175
59	=	15	390	=	200
68	=	20	440	=	225
77	=	25	480	=	250
86	=	30	530	=	275
98.6	body temp.	37	570	=	300

SPEED TABLE

MPH	KPH		MPH	KPH
6 =	10		38 =	60
13 =	20		44 =	70
19 =	30		50 =	80
25 =	40		57 =	90
31 =	50		63 =	100